Dirty River

Dirty River

A Queer Femme of Color Dreaming Her Way Home

LEAH LAKSHMI PIEPZNA-SAMARASINHA

Arsenal Pulp Press ✦ Vancouver

ARSENAL PULP PRESS
Suite 202–211 East Georgia St.
Vancouver, BC V6A 1Z6
Canada
arsenalpulp.com

The publisher gratefully acknowledges the support of the Canada Council for the Arts and the British Columbia Arts Council for its publishing program, and the Government of Canada (through the Canada Book Fund) and the Government of British Columbia (through the Book Publishing Tax Credit Program) for its publishing activities.

Cover illustration by Cristina Carrera
Design by Gerilee McBride

Printed and bound in Canada

"wrong is not yours" was previously published in
Leah Lakshmi Piepzna-Samarasinha's *Bodymap*. Toronto, ON:
Mawenzi House Publishers, 2015

Quote from "Eating Salt" by Lisa Kahaleole Hall in *Names We Call Home: Autobiography on Racial Identity,* edited by Becky Thompson and Sangeeta Tyagi (Routledge, 1996) used with permission of the author.

Library and Archives Canada Cataloguing in Publication:
Piepzna-Samarasinha, Leah Lakshmi, 1975–, author
Dirty river : a queer femme of color dreaming her way home / Leah
Lakshmi Piepzna-Samarasinha.

Issued in print and electronic formats.
ISBN 978-1-55152-600-3 (paperback).—ISBN 978-1-55152-601-0 (epub)

1. Piepzna-Samarasinha, Leah Lakshmi, 1975–. 2. Poets, Canadian (English)—21st century—Biography. 3. Sexual minority women—Canada—Biography. 4. Minority authors—Canada—Biography. I. Title.

PS8631.I46Z53 2015   C811'.6   C2015-903471-X
                                              C2015-904761-7

The Recipe

Cayenne. Turmeric. Cloves. Allspice. Cinnamon. Cardamom. Cumin. Sichuan pepper. Fennel. Curry leaf. Mustard seed. Pomegranate. Breadfruit. Sorrel. Soursop. Coconut. Cocoplum. June plum. Lime. Mango. Tamarind. Sweetsop. Carilli. Habenero pepper. Ackee n Saltfish. Jerk chicken. Ting. Peas an Rice. Shrimps. Curry Goat. Doubles. Roti. Fry Dumpling. Macaroni Pie. Crab. Snapper fish. Conch Fritters. Healing herbs. Herb garden. Vegetable gardens. The Humber River. Baby bats. Zebras. Gazelles. Sea creatures. Seashells. The ocean. Waves. Our countries. The two-thirds world. Oxygen. Breath. Breathing. Our languages. Dialect. Ebonix. Pidgin n Patois. Rastamouse. Parenting. New life. Midwives. Black kids. Black n brown kids. Di Youth Dem. Sharing. Learning. Unlearning. Unschooling. Freeschool. Africentric School. Writing. Poems. Rhythm. Building. The Movement. The Movement for Black Lives. #BlackLivesMatter. Transformation. The Transformative. LGBTT2QQ1. B(lack)I(ndigenous)POC. Thinking. Remembering. Tearing down walls to reveal our raw, bleeding, beating hearts. Healing. Fighting. Bleeding. And. Dying FREE. Reading. Getting read. Vogue. Suicide drop. Snaps.

Dancing. Jump up. Fucking. Lovers. Sweating. Moaning. Cuming. Kink. Caning. Flogging. Games. Sxting. Pussy Pulsing. Dildos. Screaming. Hardcore. Grindin. Grindin on that wood. Beyoncé. Sa-Roc. Jah Cure. Afrikan Boy. Lady Saw. LAL. Angel Haze. Ce'Cile. Tanya Stephens. G98.7. Jean Grae my blood is a million stories. The Jean Grae Show. Katt Williams. JOKES. Laughing. Kickin it on the couch. Restin. Doing nails. Enhanced eyelashes. Dog-ear fitted. Fashion. Button-downs. Mini-skirts. Hair wraps. Kicks. The Spiritual. The Stars. The Moon. Fire. Ritual. Meditation. Tarot. Catharsis. The Altar. Altered States. Rum an Juice. Spliffs. Pills. Getting carried away. Going too far. Harm reduction. Being reined back in. Being humbled. Accountability. Chatting. Chattaz. Talkin. Talkin di tings. The hair salon. The barber. Connection. Exchange. Being Alone. Being quiet. Being heard. Being seen. Being held. Soulmates. Being loved. Being in love. Loving. LOVE. COMMUNITY. FAMILY. — *LeRoi Newbold*

I love the word *survival*. It always sounds to me like a promise. It makes me wonder sometimes though, how do I define the shape of my impact upon this earth? —*Audre Lorde*

Sometimes, you're so busy surviving you forget you have.
— *David Mura*

I got guides, angels, ancestors, and homies / Pick me up when I don't know where I'm going / Home. — *Gabriel Teodros*

for all the adult runaways
and mostly, for Lisa Amin.

Contents

Part 2: Going into the Sky

Part 3: How to Come Back

Part 4: Opening/Femme like a Fist

Preface

LET'S GET SOMETHING STRAIGHT: SURVIVING ABUSE AS
CHOOSE-YOUR-OWN-ADVENTURE NOVEL

This book is not *The Courage to Heal* and it's not *Push*. It's not *When You're Ready* or *No: A Woman's Word* or any of the other brutal, pastel-covered incest books of the lesbian, feminist '70s and '80s. It's not an incest horror story book, and it's not palatable, either. In the end, I don't get normal. I get something else.

There's uplift, but it's not a straight shot. I'm not overcoming my terrible pain, my terrible, horrible, tragic lost-innocence childhood. My therapist is not a major character in it, and the therapy sessions, court dates, and talking with nice policemen, ditto.

This book is something else. It's about how running like fucking hell at twenty-one and living in an apartment with shit-gray wall-to-wall carpet, a weedy leaning tree out back, and a bunch of dandelions you eat for greens when you're broke, a yellow fluorescent light, a bathtub, and a half-busted door that doesn't completely fill the doorway but still locks can feel like paradise. Can be paradise.

The thing I always wanted to say is that surviving abuse sucks.

But it's also a choose-your-own-adventure story.

The hero(ine) sets off on a journey of lockdown, screaming at Christmas/Eid/Pesach, fucked-up yelling, a bus ticket, changing and un-listing your phone number, writing that mammoth email/letter and sending it to your parents, poverty, getting a stable girlfriend, and then everything falling apart again.

This is a road map. True romance. Leaving America, finding a one-room apartment, true brown love revolution and bullshit, finding yourself in your own body memories, chronic illness, brown sisterfemmes, homemade Diwalis, walking away, and building a new family. Not the easy way that we brown girls think about it sometimes. Those words, Family and Home, are so seductive, especially when we put Chosen in front of it. But they're not simple. Not simple at all.

It's heroic. Not heartwarming.

Throw in a little undocumented immigration, sex work, brown-on-brown domestic violence, and the struggle for social justice, plus A Portrait of the Artist as A Young Queer Brown Femme, and you've got something.

Sometimes surviving abuse isn't terrible. Sometimes, when you leave your whole life behind, it feels blissfully free. Stepping away from everything you've known. The bliss of your very first door that shuts all the way. Wind between your legs. Stopping everything that happened for seven generations.

Free. Free. Free.

Come in. Let me tell you the story.

Part 1

HOW TO RUN AWAY

1. How I Run Away from America: New York, 1997

I got on the Greyhound to Toronto at Port Authority in New York when I was twenty-one, with two backpacks, a tight black vintage slip, and a pair of fourteen-hole Docs. That was it. You only need one outfit if it's fabulous.

One of the bags was the fake-Guatemalan hot pink and lime green tote Rafael's mami had given me on my last visit to Toronto, drooling out clothes and cloth menstrual pads from its open top. The other was the massive army backpack I'd been hauling around for the past few New York years, stuffed full of textbooks and groceries from the Park Slope food co-op and pepper spray, all of it always inducing massive lumbar pain.

The backpacks held:

- *four Advil with their coatings half-eaten away in a mashed-up Altoids tin, smashed with black from cigarettes being stubbed out inside*

- *the vintage dress with chocolate brown flowers, green background, and pussy pink satin lining*

- *the hand-dyed, leaf green Mexican lace bustier that was my favorite thing to wear, scored for seven bucks at a Market clothing store*

- *a charcoal gray silk camisole, also thrifted from someplace in Kensington Market*

- *four pairs of underwear (because I was still going panty-free a lot that year)*

- *a neon turquoise and cerise paisley flowered polyester '70s skirt*

- *one other pair of jeans from Domsey's clothes-by-the-pound warehouse in Williamsburg*

- *a full set of those G-string cotton menstrual pads from Many Moons menstrual products in Victoria, British Columbia*

- *books by Chrystos, Suheir Hammad, and Audre Lorde*

- *a towel, a passport, a notebook*

The rest would stay in storage in my parents' basement in Worcester, Mass. I felt clear. Clean. I was leaving America, and this was all I needed.

Got second-staged at the border again.

"Nationality?"

"American."

The border at the Peace Bridge had a cute little clapboard house by the side of the lanes for cars with their flashing neon lights that made the border look like a disco. You got hauled off the 'hound after the driver got on the mic to say the same lecture he'd said a million times: "Take everything off the bus with you, have your identification ready, once you clear immigration come over to the side of the bus to claim your luggage, then you're going to go BACK into the building to clear Customs." This was the overnight bus to Toronto from Port Authority, 4 a.m. and the sun wasn't quite up yet. Indigo black with a line of darker blue right at the edge. It was a line of people without money, folks who rode the bus, sleepy at 4 a.m. on the graying wooden wheelchair ramp that led into the house, almost enough to make the border seem homey. But we all stood there quietly, practicing our stories in our heads. Waiting for the moment where the questions got barked at you, with all your shit spilled all over the metal table; maybe they don't like your papers, maybe you get sent back.

It was always a trick, trying to rearrange my face while I was standing in line, trying to make bedhead and crusty eyes look respectable. It was all about rearranging my face to look like an arty, middle-class kid on vacation, careless, like I had plenty of money and credit cards in my army bag. Trying to look like I was the guy behind the counter's daughter, or something he wanted to fuck, or someone he didn't want to fuck who was therefore unimportant.

And then there was the matter of which guy behind the counter you angled for. There was a science in trying to figure out whether to hope for the older, potbellied Archie Bunker or the early-twenties model to his right. The older ones barked, "Where d'ya live? Where are you going? For how long?" but didn't give as much of a shit; the younger ones were more obvious about wanting to fuck you, but were also more nervous about doing their job right and likely to pull you over if they weren't completely sure. All of us stood in that predawn light, squinting and leaning forward to try to see our choices without being too obvious, while thinking over our strategy and tactics—whirring fast behind all those tense foreheads—trying to look relaxed and casual. You didn't actually have any choice of border guard; it would look weird saying, "Oh, no, you go ahead," in the immigration line, but we tried.

This time I'd drawn Archie. He looked just like a Boston cop—big spare tire, iron gray stubble hair cut—just with a little more Ontario British lilt in his voice. I tried to breathe. Picked up my bags, walked up to the scratched-up Plexiglas window, and slid my passport through the slot. "Good morning, how are you?" Trying to sound smooth, but my voice was still too high and squeaky.

He looked at my passport, then at me. What did he see? A frizzy-curly-haired girl with light brown skin (could be so many things), carrying an old US passport that had been through the wash, wearing a leather jacket, tight slip, jeans with holes in the knees, voice high and tight, looking back at him with bleary, milky eyes.

"Purpose of visit?"

"To visit my fiancé." Smile brightly. *Please, oh please, don't look in my bag.* How do fiancées look? Do fiancées have big-ass dildos and a box of gloves from the HIV street outreach job shoved in the bottom of their army backpack? Who the fuck gets married at twenty-one? Who looks like me and is married? And what finger was the ring supposed to go on, anyway?

"Where does he live?"

"Toronto."

"*Where* in Toronto?"

"Dupont and Lansdowne." The intersection known for the toilet factory, the high rise where Rafael lived with its STUDIO APARTMENTS FOR $400. PAY YOUR DEPOSIT IN MONTHLY INSTALL-MENTS sign, the Big Wrecks towing company, and a crackhead Coffee Time branch down below.

"What's his name?"

"Rafael Vidal-Garza."

I could see the shit hitting the fan, right on the dude's big-ass steel aviator frames.

"Step over there, please."

"Sure."

Look eager. Look a little puzzled but compliant. Look like you've never done anything wrong in your life.

I chanted it to myself as dude led me over to the big steel table, like the gynecologist's table from hell. But I couldn't quite manage it. I was shaking and pale, my voice was tremoring and I knew that they could tell I was wrong, a liar, sneaking into their country to plot the anarchist–First Nations–Kensington

Market revolution with two bags full of sex toys and some hoochie dresses. And maybe was a ho too. Which was what I'd planned. I'd chatted with Amber, my mentor at the Lesbian AIDS Project where I interned, about how I wasn't going to go on to grad school, I was going to move to Toronto, work on the prison justice paper and do 'net porn. It was a fine and honored career path for girls like me, whoever they were.

"Put your belongings down here." It was the younger guy. Archie Bunker had nodded him over from where he was covertly gaping at my tits to go do search and rescue. He snapped on the rubber gloves, and I had a flashback to the hundreds of Lesbian Safer Sex pamphlets with the gloved fist on the cover that I'd handed out on Pride Day. Things were moving slow like molasses here, and all I could think of was Kristina's cock buried in the bottom of the backpack below the lube, the condoms, the other hoochie dress, and all my underwear. *Maybe he'll stop before he gets there. Maybe I don't look like a ho,* standing there in a couple days' worth of musk and my slip.

But he was thorough. He methodically worked his way down through the dresses and the underwear, picking up the Altoids tin and looking at the ash and the mottled pills.

"What are these?"

"Advil."

"They don't look like any Advil I've ever seen."

"They got wet and the coating got eaten off. You can throw them out if you want, I don't care."

"Okay. Have you ever been arrested? If you're honest with

me, it'll be fine. But if you lie, I'll find out and you'll be in big trouble."

The classic cop throwdown. I flashed to Rafael repeating what cops always said to him when they stopped him for not having a light on his bike or slowing, not stopping, at a stop sign: *We can do this the easy way, or we can do this the hard way. We could kill you and make it look like an accident. No one would know. No one would even care.*

But what if they really did have everything in their damn computer? What if they knew already? Then again, what if they didn't, and I'd give away a crucial piece of info to the one-world government? But they had fingerprinted me at the squat bust in May, and they'd done it before then at the shut-down-the-city, anti-Giuliani demo. Too late.

"Once. But it was for disturbing the peace, at a demonstration."

"What kind of demonstration?"

"Oh, a student one. Against a tuition hike." *Arty girls with money sometimes protest tuition hikes, right?* Better to say that than to try to describe the demonstration I'd been arrested at where a motley, beautiful coalition of ACT UP-ers, Asians Against Police Brutality, and the CUNY student coalition had managed to sit down in traffic and shut down all four bridges and tunnels leading out of Manhattan, at rush hour on the day Giuliani released his budget destroying all funding for AIDS-related programming as well as hiking tuition, and funding tons more cops to enforce "quality of life" laws that would bust you for being homeless. The mayor had been really pissed, and we'd all been kept in jail for three days, not the couple of hours the white-guy ACT UP veterans assured us was standard.

"Okay." He stared at me. He was kind of cute for a white boy. Soft brown eyes, brown hair that was growing out a little from his crewcut. How old was he? A few years older than me? He didn't look evil, no more than any other twenty-three-year-old white guy. Who decides that working for the border is the way to go in their early twenties, though?

He started going through the bag again, emptying out each piece of clothing in its coating of tobacco dust and cat hair. And, *oh shit*, he wasn't seeing anything that made him want to stop. I decided to speak up.

"Um," I said then, with more of a purr, "Um, sir?" I peered from behind my lashes.

He looked up, irritated. "What?"

"Um, there's something really embarrassing in the bottom of that bag!" I chirped. I sounded just like a Spice girl wet dream, five years too early.

"Oh yeah? What's that?"

"Uh, well." *C'mon, make this good.* "A friend of mine is getting married, and she's having a bridal shower. We were all supposed to bring a, um, gag gift, and, um … "

At that moment, his fingers closed around my dick at the bottom of the bag. I watched his face go through a couple of contortions. *What the—oh my god, its a cock, holy shit, it's bigger than mine.* I saw disgust mixing with an instant boner.

He blinked. Straightened up and didn't look at me. "That's all, miss. You can get back on the bus now."

I climbed back on the bus. "They sure kept you for a long time," one lady said.

"Yeah," I said. I set my bags down, took off my jacket, and scrunched it up for a pillow. My body was all corded up, tense, like I'd been clenching all my muscles for an hour. But now, I could feel it softening. My whole body was letting out one big exhale as the bus shuddered awake and groaned forward. I'd made it. We'd passed over that invisible line on the map. The trees were greener, the air was less polluted, the signs were in kilometers not miles, and I was rushing to that safe place in my head, with Rafael's big grin, our twin plum-colored futon on the floor, café con leche in chipped tiny cups in the morning, a hand on my ass and around my waist—and my parents, America, and everything bad thousands of miles away.

2. 1996, Summer of Love

How it starts is: I'm supposed to go on an anarchist vacation, but my boyfriend doesn't show up. So I go by myself, and I don't come back.

New York activist culture 1996 was five to ten meetings a week, coffee and a pack of Camels and you don't need any sleep, what's wrong with you? It was all-day CUNY Coalition meetings on Saturdays at the Grad Center with representatives from every student group in New York battling it out, the broke-ass Black and Latina/o reps from CCNY and Hunter and the fired-up Student Liberation Action Movement members who organized a citywide walkout against Giuliani's plans to destroy public education and got over 10,000 students to City Hall, some in junior high, some in grade school. It's one older woman with iron gray hair standing up when we're on hour seven of the meeting shouting that she's a Stalinist, and if we all followed Stalin, everything would be fine. It's a slice, a coffee, breakfast at three a.m. beer and cigarettes are all you need.

In New York, people ask you how you're doing and don't want to know the answer. We plan crazyamazing actions, like dropping a giant condom with "Condom use saves lives: ACT

UP" from the side of the Waldorf Astoria when the pope is visiting. I can't get arrested at that one, because I've already been arrested at two protests in the past two months, unlike the other activists who dress up in their nicest clothes and eat at the Waldorf restaurant so they can rush to the windows and drop the banner they've smuggled in as soon as the pope is underneath. Instead, I tuck as much of my hair as I can into a bun, put on a long flowered dress, and hang out at the makeup floor for hours, drifting around with a walkie-talkie hidden in my purse, trying on samples and keeping an eye out for cops rushing the elevators.

Alexio was a super-sweet, super-shy boy with thirty-eight earrings, hair to his butt, and no money. He was from Fall River, a fucked-up Massachusetts mill town similar to Worcester. He was sort of my boyfriend. Not really a boyfriend; more like a guy who'd walked into the anarchist bookstore on Avenue B where I volunteered and actually seemed not to be an asshole. Who'd then been at the same anarchist conference at Antioch I'd taken a bus to in order to escape the person I'd been dating, who looked like Freddie Krueger as a queeny fag with a million skull tattoos, one for every one of his friends who'd died of AIDS. Freddie had started calling me from the infoshop phone every five minutes, threatening to kill me, after some combination of a helmet-free bike accident on the Williamsburg Bridge and reverting to heroin had ended the honeymoon stage of our relationship.

Me and Alexio had hooked up in one of the cabins at the anarchist conference, after the soysage and the women's circle and the demos of how to un-arrest people. He'd been really embarrassed because he had a huge cock, and his first girlfriend had been a punk rock debutante who loved Andrea Dworkin and made him feel like, if all penetration was rape, his cock was a war crime.

We'd stayed in touch since. He was the guy I'd take the bus to see in Boston when things got hairy in New York, and I wanted to walk around under some trees, go to a housing-rights demonstration, and sleep with a cute boy-man under 3,000 thrift-stored blankets that somehow still didn't cover the bed but kept us warm. I'd go to his collective house in Allston, the one where he was the only one without a trust fund, and rest up.

The plan that summer was that he was going to hitchhike all over the lower twenty states by himself and then come up to New York in August, and we'd hit the road together. Go see my best friend Allison from the Riot Grrl listserv who was moving to Toronto from Kitchener-Waterloo, Ontario, to live in the Anti-Racist Action house now that she'd finished school. (I was too socially awkward and depressed to have real, in-person friends in New York, but damn, I sure could type.) Then go to the Trumbullplex in Detroit, one of those world-famous squats you read about in anarchist magazines, a huge mansion in the Detroit wasteland covered in murals and community gardens. Then we'd go to Chicago and get our heads smashed in at the protests outside the '96 Democratic National Convention, the ones those folks at the Antioch anarchist conference had been learning un-arrest techniques in preparation for.

I was still living in Brooklyn that summer, going to work

at my internship at the Lesbian AIDS Project during the day, coming home at night to the fourth-floor walkup apartment at Dean and Flatbush where I'd been living for the past year. It was sunny and empty; the Anarchist Bi Girl House had been a collective failure of a collective house, and no one was around very much.

The landlord at 476 Dean Street had taken this once-spacious one-bedroom with dining room and stuck in two prefab walk-in closets from Home Depot. Then he'd hacked some two by fours into loft beds, smacked a skylight into the top, and there it was, a three-bedroom, and he could triple the rent. We lived in the closets, an irony that was lost on none of us. It didn't make for much privacy, but it cost $300 a month, and it was better than other situations that folks I knew in New York were holding down, like paying $500 to sleep on a couch.

I came home every day to Dave, the career Revolutionary Communist Party dude who was in the student movement with me and everyone else in the house. He was not an Anarchist Bi Girl, he was a dude whose parents had been in the RCP; he'd practically been born into it. They'd been sent to live in a small Kentucky town to organize the workers and were the only Jews around for hundreds of miles. Dave had supposedly been thrown out of the party for playing "Irresistible Bitch" by Prince on the Revolution Books sound system. The official charge was "bourgeois decadence" and also woman-hating, although he'd tried to explain that the song was really about a woman who controlled men and got whatever she wanted—didn't they get it? He'd been living in a supplies cabinet at CUNY for a while, keeping his one Armani suit pressed and hanging in the corner (because a man always has to have one good suit), but that had gotten a little tired and he'd moved in to the Dean Street house when my roommate Jacqui moved out. He lived in the walk-in closet next to mine.

I would stagger up in the morning, trying to make it to my hair control-product lineup in the bathroom, and there would be Dave, impeccably clean-shaven with a tight fade and manic little commie eyes, sipping an espresso with a twist of lemon and reading Hegel at our kitchen table at 7:30 in the morning. And as I'd stagger out from the bathroom with the hair-control product lineup, trying to make my hair look like the good, brown-girl curly hair I saw every five seconds on the block but had no idea how to achieve as a mixed-race girl who'd had a white mom with a hairbrush problem, he'd try to debate freaking Hegel with me as I toasted food-co-op whole wheat and made the Bustelo.

I was spending my evenings reading Cherrie Moraga's "The Breakdown of the Bicultural Mind," over and over in my narrow, twin loft bed, up by the ceiling painted blue with smears of white like clouds, and I had close to no interest in Hegel. Dave and I didn't get along. Early on, Dave had scanned the line of books on my tiny bookshelf, at the spines of *This Bridge Called My Back* and *Angry Woman* and every book Sapphire had written and sneered, "Wow, there's absolutely nothing in there that I'd want to read." We'd already had a fight over religion: opiate of the masses or liberation through grounded earth-based spirituality like they had in the Bay Area?

In the mornings, I'd haul my backpack on and take the 2

Train to the Lesbian AIDS Project office at Gay Men's Health Crisis, where I worked that summer. Go inside the office dividers. Type in Windows 95 green screen. Try to give out dental dams to the ladies who came to the socials, who weren't using them even if they and their lovers were both positive, because if you were going to die anyway, you might as well be able to feel your lover's tongue on your pussy.

I didn't know what I was going to do when I graduated from Eugene Lang College, back when it only cost $12,000 a year and they had plenty of financial aid for first-time students of color. I made five dollars under the table an hour working at the health food store or at LAP. My old roommate Samantha temped in offices and made eight dollars an hour, and we thought that was a lot of money. Every year, there was more gentrification of the neighborhoods we lived in, more moving further out from Manhattan and a longer commute. When I'd moved into my first apartment at Avenue B and East Second, I paid $280 a month, and I could walk to school. Now I was contemplating a move out to Lefrak City, Queens, which would mean a three-hour commute to get to school.

And more than that. I didn't have any friends. I didn't know how to talk about so many things. Like how depressed I felt all the time. "Depression" didn't seem like a big enough word to describe the crazy. I couldn't feel my body, and I couldn't make friends. Getting up in the mornings was a struggle. I needed to sleep fourteen hours a day. Talking to people felt overwhelming. My mother had raised me on, "Just wait til you get to college; there will be people like you there," and it was sort of true, but I still didn't know how to talk to them. I had grown up in blue-collar wilderness, and I ran the fuck away to go to someplace where I couldn't see the sky between the towers. It wasn't working out so good. I thought I would have Community, but it hadn't quite worked out that way.

Hitchhiking around America sounded good. The problem was that, as much as I liked reading zines written by other people who'd done it, there were a lot of days when just walking down the street in Brooklyn was challenging enough for me. I wasn't sure how being all by myself by the side of the road in Iowa was gonna work out if sometimes all the "Hey, baby!"s and hisses and dudes trying to follow me up the stairs to my house made me stay inside my apartment.

You remember those boys who had dialers? I don't know how it worked, but they simulated the sound of dimes falling, and if you held one up to a pay phone, you could call anywhere in the US for free. Alexio had a dialer, and he was supposed to call me from Alabama and all the other places in the South he was hitchhiking through and update me about how it was going. But the months went by, and the call just never came. And when the call never came, I wanted a vacation anyway. *Fuck it. I'll go by myself. I'll just take the bus.*

3. Girlbomb

There's nothing like being young, brown, queer, in love, and completely insane.

Me and Rafael fucking in the middle of a field, twenty-one years old, in the middle of a music festival, green milky august grass stems humming birds insects so, so super sweet, *if we ever have a child can we make her here,* I want to, we got a ride up on the bus, my tiny bright orange and lime green gingham mini-dress that stops right under the ass, him coming up and leaning me into the bus and making out with me, us being that crazy brown couple holding knives and taking pictures in the collective festival kitchen, his Malcolm X shirt, my horny grin, fucking and nonstop talking, slept next to each other on a twin futon mattress on the floor every day and it never felt crowded, me and him meeting talking nonstop sex race class abuse and crazy, at KOS back when it was the diner on the corner, mixed-race brown, our parents, the movements, me and him walking home walking his bike from the Anti-Racist Action house where we've worn out our welcome fucking on the floor every night for four days in a row and staying up all night watching *Brother from Another Planet* on video, walking his bike from the ARA house at Markham and College to his shitty bachelor apartment at Dupont and Lansdowne, when I ask him how long he says, "not far," but it's a couple hours, we stop to fuck under the jungle gym in the playground a block away from the ARA house, hear someone breathing hard, look up, it's some slimy gross fiftyish white man with his dick in his hand and Rafael jumps up, pulls his knife out of his pants, screaming, "I kill people like you!" he's triggered shaking out of it out of his body and I am familiar with that trigger I am familiar with him his body his survivor self the way his eyes look when he ain't here and he's familiar with mine too, we are survivor brown queer fucking true love soulmates, he is the kind of boyfriend anyone's mother will shiver thinking her daughter is fucking, maybe, we walk home slowly past Christie Pits, past what he calls Little Aztlan but it's Toronto so it's like one pupusa place and two Latino groceries next to the park, nothing is gentrified nothing is what I recognize, shit is not fixed up it's dusty smog-covered East African restaurants, little fruit and veggie stands, doughnut shops with crackheads staying up late, broke people bars with BEER $2 written in marker on a piece of brown cardboard in the window, it's like Europe it's preserved under a layer of dust, and when we stop at the Doughnut City an hour into our shamble, and my legs and hips and ass ache and we're still not home, and ask for doughnuts, the guy pulls a box out from under the counter, we look and see all the doughnuts on the racks are plastic—it's a numbers-running joint. We laugh, we keep walking.

And finally make it home to the two towers with BACHELORS

$400 PAY YOUR FIRST AND LAST IN MONTHLY INSTALLMENTS giant banner on the side of one, security guards and attack dog and pepper spray behind bulletproof glass in the foyer. There are two elevators, one is working. We wait. Rafael lives on the fifth floor in a one-room with one giant window. Put down the café con leche, there are ten roaches floating in it five minutes later. It has a tiny bathroom, a two-burner stove that gives electrical shocks—threw me across the room once—and posters everywhere, The Angry Brigade, George Jackson, Assata Shakur, and a wall lined with milk-crate bookcases. We drink warm dollar-store peppermint tea and eat ginger bulla, rice and beans, six bagels for a buck from the Price Chopper. This is all I need: fucking, tea, reading to each other from *Aloud: Voices from the Nuyorican Poets Cafe*, boom box with GZA RZA, all the Wu Tang greatest hits plus Nina Simone, the Congos, and old, old Marley.

Sometimes, women are attracted to dangerous men.

Sometimes we're attracted to them because our whole lives have been so dangerous, we don't even recognize danger when we see it.

Sometimes, we choose dangerous lovers cause they feed us something we ain't getting from any other source.

Sometimes, we're attracted to them because that kind of crazy feels familiar. Not the crazy of abusive, but the crazy of us. The crazy of our own brains, except with the masculines, the crazy is some kinda Tupac, Dylan, Che, Kerouac, some kind of romantic, wandering hotshot Mad Max troubadour amazement. It's sexy. We don't think it's going to be a mess.

Sometimes, we want one hell of an adventure
and they want us because cray recognizes cray
and at least whatever happens, it won't be boring.

Toronto in 1996 was abandonedpretty. A downtown that hadn't become the New Urbanism yet. An underground not yet commercialized, sanitized into a target market. When we walked down Queen Street West to Parkdale, there were miles of empty and broke. Not picturesque broke, but broke-broke. Across from Trinity Bellwoods Park there was an old house abandoned in the middle of a wild field of flowers and grasses three feet high; it had been allowed to be abandoned in the middle of downtown. Now it's renovated, gated, and surrounded by loftominiums on both sides, but then there were empty factories, anachronistic men's fine clothing stores, by-the-week residential hotels, kitchen supply warehouses, and tons of storefronts that sold stolen bikes. On one walk home, Rafael and I fucked in the middle of that field as folks walked by unconcerned, ten feet away.

Abandonedpretty, and it was easy to feel like downtown could just detach. The First Nations Sovereignty / Ontario Coalition Against Poverty / mad queer POC rebellion would happen, and we would just secede. It made more sense to me than hoping that all the fringe revolutionary lefty parties would unite and overthrow the government. It would be like in *The Fifth Sacred Thing*; things would fall apart—the environment, the systems, everything, and a lot of people would die. Good people. A lot more people would end up in some prison camps somewhere. But then there would be people who would be lucky enough to end up in some area where, by luck and randomness, there would be freedom. Toronto could be like that. It made more sense to trust in chaos than to trust in the rational.

I'd borrow Rafael's clothes, his Dacajawea and Malcolm X T-shirts with the sleeves cut all the way out, only on me, they showed my tits and my black lace bra. Sometimes I'd wear the big navy blue pair of coveralls splashed with paint and wheat paste and walk down the block bopping my ass, the top of the coveralls unzipped and tied around my waist to reveal my tiny black tank top, and as long as I was walking with this meathead homeboy, nobody was going to say a goddamn thing to me.

The days were a rapture of waking up cuddled up to that brown body with its hand on my ass, a two-hour snuggle, an hour of drinking café con leche, then maybe two hours of sex followed by a long, slow rapturous walk to a meeting or food gathering, and then walking back home. We stayed up drinking peppermint tea and reading, fucking, listening to CKLN-FM, Ryerson's campus-community radio station, always on the fucked-up tiny boom box with two cassette players or all of Rafael's mixtapes with Massive Attack, African Head Charge, Tricky, Marvin Gaye, Rita Marley, and the Fugees. We loved the '70s. It was $1.99-brown-cane-sugar-chunks-from-the-West-Indian-aisle-at-Price-Chopper sweet.

Rafael ran away from home when he was fourteen. His dad beat him and his mother every day, or at least when his dad was around. Rafael's parents both had university degrees from

Chile. His father was the first generation to scrape from the village to the university; his mama came from a more stable middle-class Isla Negra family. When they had to flee Chile after Pinochet destroyed the revolution, Canada laughed at their degrees. They had to go back to school to get Canadian degrees so they could get Canadian jobs, sitting through classes they'd already taken and gotten As in. Rafael's father had worked three jobs. Sometimes he didn't sleep for weeks, was how Rafael remembered it. When Rafael ran away, he got taken in by the punk scene. He'd slept in doorways and bridges and squats like Fort Goof, sold weed, and signed up at temp factory-job places. He dumpstered the food Kensington Market stalls left out after they shuttered at night.

He had boyfriends and girlfriends, although the first girl he'd fucked—the one he'd asked out by giving her a Sex Pistols button outside the show at the Reverb—had yelled "Wrong hole, asshole!" at him when they'd tried to do it the first time. He'd volunteered for Prison News Service, the prison justice/poor people's First Nations/psych survivor free paper that we left on buses and at corner stores so people could pick it up for free, and been with ARA since the beginning. He hung out with West Side Crew and the ARA kids and the crazies til he smashed in a McDonald's window during Toronto's version of the L.A. rebellion—the photo had made the front page of the paper— and he'd had to get out of town for a while. He'd stayed in Vancouver, where his parents lived, and started to see them, guardedly. A lot of the time, Rafael and his father would start to hit each other halfway through the meal. Then he'd come back to Toronto, gotten arrested, done his month at the Don Jail for the smash-up, and gotten out, a prison activist.

We had had some of the same experiences, and we bitched about them together on the long walks to and from CKLN to do Prison News Service radio or the Monday night edition of Word of Mouth, the six to seven p.m. news slot.

"So, we're in the meeting, and somebody's, like, how come there are no people of color here if we're an anti-racist group? And some moron pipes up with, 'Well, Rafael is a person of color, I guess!' And then this guy, he goes, 'And I'm Jewish!' and it drives me insane! He thinks he's doing me a favor, but it's not the same thing! Just 'cause you're not some vegan from Richmond Hill doesn't mean you're not white. How come the cops always know I'm not white but then these fuckers don't?"

I nodded vigorously. "Yeah, there was this one time in Blackout Books where I tried to bring up that they were helping gentrify the neighborhood because everyone was white but me, and this one guy laughed, and then a second guy said, 'But, Leah, we're all anarchists; of course we're against racism!' "

It was kind of like paying to be in jail to live in Rafael's apartment. The security guards at the entrance smirked at us when we walked in, me with my hickies and Rafael with his cocky bluster. One time, we were making out in front of the one elevator that worked and one of them got on the mic and said, "Hey, buddy, go fuck your girl upstairs." Rafael turned around, stared at him for twenty seconds, and then very deliberately gave him the finger. The elevator showed up at that moment, and we stepped inside and started kissing again. However, after three storeys, the elevator started to go back down. The doors opened and the dude was sitting there, all squatty-frog five-foot-six of him, holding the attack dog in one hand and the pepper spray in the other. "Hey, buddy," he said to Rafael, "I was talking to you!" Rafael actually looked like he was going to fight him for a second but realized it wouldn't be a good idea and backed off. We walked the five flights up.

Sometimes you do shit that doesn't make a lot of sense to anybody but you, but it's all lit up. You just know. Why move to Canada? Rafael is all lit up. This is the one, the boyman that I'm going to be with for the rest of my life. The answer to what I'm doing after I graduate. The one who is not just love, but the mixed-brown-survivor-separated-at-birth brother I've been looking for.

4. Running Away Root

I started wanting to run away when I was seven. I had this little red suitcase with a rainbow on it from Caldor's Department Store, very '70s. I packed it with *Tales of a Fourth Grade Nothing*, some shirts and underwear, and announced that I was going.

Most parents would laugh, or say, *Go right ahead*, or get angry and send you to your room. My mother started to cry. Deep sobs, heaving like she was going to throw up. Then she ran to the bedroom and threw herself on the bed.

Was this one of the times when she didn't speak to me for a couple of days? Something my mother said a lot was, "I don't have to hit you like my parents did to me. I just stop loving you for a few days, and you fall right in line."

I don't remember. But my love of books about kids who ran away continued. I bought my favorite, *The Runaway's Diary*, in paperback after wearing out the copy from the public library. It's a book about a teenage girl, kind of a tomboy butch, who runs away from Harrisburg, Pennsylvania in the 1960s and hitchhikes to a quiet green place full of trees somewhere in eastern Quebec. She talks a lot to her diary. She doesn't talk to almost anybody else. She gets a dog. There's some mandatory boy crush in there, but mostly she's a dyke, they just don't say so.

All of this made my mother cry, a lot.

It was hard to describe what was wrong at my house.

My dad was mostly either not there or making everyone cringe in fear when he was there. He made us both cry a lot.

My mom was more complicated. Sometimes she was the best mom ever, better than any other mom. My ally. My buddy. The one who said weird girls were just fine, and when I grew up and went to college I would be fine too. More like a friend than a mom. My best friend.

But then there were other times. Like those times. There was the stuff. Like how our doors were locked, our blinds were drawn. Like how we lived on a dead-end street, and I wasn't allowed to walk off the block because "I'd get raped out there." Like how she had it timed how long it took to walk to the mailbox that was ten yards off the end of the street, and if I didn't get home in that time, she'd be weeping and crying and shaking, "How could you do this to me?" Like how I wasn't allowed to close my bedroom door, how she would brush my hair straight and get angry when I asked what color I was, we were.

And there was something deeper and weirder that I hadn't yet figured out. But she was my mom. She was the good one.

When I was a kid, I remember looking at my parents and thinking, *I love you, but you're really fucked up. And when I grow up, I'm going to do something else.*

5. Some Notes about the Going Away: or, You Are a Twenty-Two-Year-Old Brown Slutty Girl Who Thinks Maybe You're an Incest Survivor Reading *The Courage to Heal* Standing Up in the Bookstore

When I was in New York, I discovered the pleasures of reading standing up in the bookstore aisle. I didn't have a lot of money, and I couldn't figure out the library system. I'd pictured New York libraries to be better than the best, definitely better than Worcester's, but there were just a few of them, and they were often closed for renovations for years, and all the books I wanted always seemed to have been stolen anyways.

But what New York did have was bookstores that stayed open til midnight, and there were enough of them that I could circulate, reading standing up for hours at a time til they closed without arousing too much suspicion. Tower Books had a big drug and sex aisle; Shakespeare & Company had literary magazines and small press books and nice-smelling wood walls; St. Mark's had tons of zines and a small, furtive People of Color section; and all of them were a half-hour walk from my house. I had a mental map of all the stores and I knew their hours, so if things got to be too much on the street where I was walking with my cigarette and my furious thoughts, I could duck in for a break.

I would go to the women's studies and queer studies sections and stand there reading whatever book I was working on that week. But I circled the Abuse Survivor sections like a hawk. It could take me an hour or two to actually sidle up to where it was, but I would make it there eventually, especially at Shakespeare & Company, where it was right at the base of the staircase that lead into the basement, in a little nook, like they'd figured out that people didn't want to be seen standing there.

I'd pick up *The Courage to Heal* and hold it in my arms like a thick boyfriend. I'd stolen a copy from the library back home, cutting out the security tag and putting it in my backpack, because I didn't want to face the library checkout person with a big book about incest. The pages would fall open to where the text was marked with a box or laid out in bullet points. *When you were a child, were you fondled, kissed or held for an adult's sexual pleasure? Were you touched genitally while being bathed?* I don't remember. *It is common for children to cope with abuse by forgetting it ever happened. You may have repressed vast chunks of your childhood.*

So yeah, I'd had some flashbacks and shit. I didn't know what to call them, but I couldn't feel my legs or my body or anything, really. I would look down and think, *That's my leg. What does it mean, that's my leg?* It freaked me out.

I would flip through the pages, and they all were so damn familiar. A voice in my head was going *yes, yes, yes, yes.* When you see your whole life, everything that makes it up, written in the stars or in the pages of a book, it's like seeing a map to what is you. Okay, some of the shit I didn't relate to, but that checklist, yes. And a lot of things that weren't on the checklist. The way my pussy would close or bleed. The way I would be all horny but then rise up and away, close my eyes and see the yellow walls of the bedroom I had in our first house in Watertown, where I lived before the age of four. The tiny pink small feeling I'd have that I called "my baby feeling." The way I hated myself so actively it was like a job I worked at full time. The way I split. The way I wasn't allowed to shut the door to my room, the way my mom grabbed my ass, the way my mom said we were more like best friends than mom and daughter? The way the house was all locked up, the way she said *Carrie* was her favorite movie after *Alien*, because the mom reminded her of her mom?

But what if I was just born fucked up? What if, as my mom had said, some kids are just born this way, born oversensitive, crazy, full of storm-cloud child rages and open treetop, head-ripped lightning? Just born that way, and I was making this up as a convenient excuse for all my weaknesses.

You want there to be a video in the attic of the abuse. You hit play, and it's all there, signed and dated. You'd know.

It doesn't happen that way. But even if you were crazy little when whatever went down did, it's everywhere, in the breath of air behind the windows in your house that your mama won't let you open.

6. Piece of My Heart: Queer Women of Color

I could say that I moved to Toronto because rent was $450 for a place with a porch and a front garden and the minimum wage was nine dollars an hour, twice as much as in New York. That there were arts grants that people you knew had gotten, that there was free health care. That I moved for love, or Sri Lankans, or to get away from my family, or all of the above. And all of the above would be true. But it is also true that I moved for queer women of color.

In Toronto in 1996 there was all this queer women of colo(u)r stuff. Toronto was the place where that book I'd found in Shakespeare & Company and held on to for dear life, *Miscegenation Blues: Voices of Mixed Race Women*, was published and where it seemed like most of the people in it were from. They seemed to know each other.

Women of color, Toronto-style, meant Black—African-Canadian, Afro-Caribbean, and continental African. It meant South Asian in all its forms, from all parts of the sub-continent and Caribbean and diaspora. It meant Latin American, Arab, and North African. It meant all kinds of Asian. It was everyone from a recently decolonized country, every refugee and immigrant, everyone America hadn't let in because they didn't have enough money or green card points, but Canada had, and First Nations women from here, from this non-decolonized country. Sister Vision Press, the Canadian version of Kitchen Table: Women of Color Press, ran Sistah's Cafe, a queer women of color cafe at Queen and Ossington. They bought land they called Camp Sis, queer women of color land, about three hours outside Toronto. I'd picked up a copy of *Bamboo Girl* from Adult Crash, the punk record, CD, and zine store run by Asians on Avenue A and 5th. In one of the first issues, Sabrina Margarita recounted her road trip from New York to Toronto, where she'd heard there was a queer Pinay women's group, Babaylan, some of whom were punk.

Mostly it was this: that there was this place where people were talking, out loud, about a queer/woman of color feminism, culture, and community. And it was mixed. It had South Asians in it. And it was anti-colonial. And it was APIA and Arab and Native and Black. In New York in 1996 hardly anyone was talking talked about Asian anything. There were two South Asian groups I knew of in the whole city, the South Asian Lesbian and Gay Association and the South Asian domestic violence group, SAKHI, but they felt so liberal, so different from all the student-of-color radicals I was rioting in the streets with and shoving blood-smeared copies of the *New York Times* financial section into Chase ATMs the day Mexico declared war on the Zapatistas. There was no Asians Against Police Brutality. There were maybe two or three other South Asians I knew of in the student movement against Giuliani and Pataki and prisons.

Nobody knew where Sri Lanka was. Being mixed was barely on the map, even though it was everywhere on every map.

I went looking for my people based on a book. And I found them. I found Women against Racist Policing (WARP), Toronto Coalition Against Racism (TCAR), which had a bland as hell name but was Lankan, Native, Afro-Caribbean, Afro-Canadian, continental African, and Pakistani. Where you could ask, "Indian Mohammad or Eritrean Mohammad?" and it was totally normal. I found A Different Booklist, maybe North America's only queer of color bookstore, run by Wesley and his boyfriend Johnny. The Franz Fanon and Patrick Califia books sat next to each other and Rafael and I would hang out all day long, reading all the books standing up, drinking bottomless cups of free coffee, and eating sweet potato pone that Johnny's mother had made. I found a feminism of color that predated INCITE in the United States by ten years—a feminism of color that was truly multicultural and multi-generational, that was Anishnaabe and Palestinian and Lankan and Egyptian-Jewish, Roma, Trinidadian, Ghanian, Mohawk, and Chilean. A feminism of color where we listened to Chrystos, Makeda Silvera, and Patrick Califia share a stage in an auditorium at Ryerson University that held 400 people, packed full.

In 1997, Edmund Yu was shot to death by the cops in the Spadina streetcar where it pulled up at King Street, the end of the line. "Crazy" Chinese guy, he acted in a way the other folks on the streetcar got scared of and they called the cops. He held up the tiny hammer he used to crack nuts with, and the cops shot him. The Coalition against Racist Police Violence marched up Spadina and then over to Queen's Park. Black and brown people, no permit, First Nations women singing the "Strong Woman Song." Then we walked over to the Toronto police headquarters, where the cops rode horses into the crowd. Rafael and Anna and I went to Alicia's house at the Dykeominiums, a cluster of apartments down by Parliament and Dundas, to make spanakopita. We flirted, all three of us, and Rafael grinned nervously. Safiya Bukkhari and Ramona Afrika from the MOVE organization came up from Philly and spoke at the Unitarian church, and we cooked tons of food for them. Rafael asked me if I really wanted to wear my short orange and green mini-dress to the MOVE speak, because I should think of what kind of impression it would make. Our Eric Drooker wall calendar was full of meetings, radio shows to prep for, benefits, and parties, seventeen meetings a week sometimes, and we walked miles to them and back because we never had bus fare. We were always going to the provincial or federal court for somebody's case. Rafael would tell the guards that his do-rag was religious headgear so he could keep it on. Sometimes it worked.

But around me always was the phrase queer women of color, making things possible. Making me possible. Making things possible like Desh Pardesh, the radical queer South Asian arts and politics festival, run by queers, with almost every kind of desi, the place that would in a few years be the first place that ever paid me to read poetry. *At the Crossroads* magazine, Karen Miranda Augustine's Black feminist art newspaper. Counting Past 2, the trans festival that Metis trans sex worker organizer Mirha Soleil Ross started, that she ran on many cans of Jolt cola and trans Native women's genius. The meetings in laundromats and Black and brown women's houses where we plotted to get tampons and cash to women in prison. And the more informal meetings, the ones outside a tiny club smoking cigarettes, in Chinese bakeries and at the food pantry, where we smoked and talked shit and stared at each other.

I was raised here. By these women-of-color places that taught me that being a light-skinned person was a privilege and a tax, that it didn't mean you were prettier or more special than anyone else, it meant you took your privilege and went in and got the grant or stole the spray paint because no one was following you around the store, and then you shared the money and spray paint with everyone. By this Black, Indigenous, and women-of-color solidarity, that said we were on stolen, unceded land lifted up by Black and immigrant women's un- and under-paid and deported labor, that our work was about all the ways we could decolonize our minds, our hair, our hearts, together. The way the Toronto Women's Bookstore, taken over by queer women of color, let me read *Caucasia* and Suheir Hammad's new book of poetry standing up, for hours, without comment, always saying hi. By all the punks of color who left and started women-of-color collectives that took all the good in DIY and wove it with how our Black and brown families had always been DIY.

My mama didn't raise me right, but I tried to raise myself that way. And I didn't raise myself alone. You raised me.

7. The Punk Kid of Color Clusterfuck

There were always one or two or three kids of color in any given scene, somewhere. Word would spread about the existence of certain clusters. *Kristen, she's Vietnamese, she's in Anti-Racist Action in Toronto. Him, I wonder about him, he's mixed, yeah. There's that one Black punk girl in* _____ (yeah, that's fill in the blank). And those cities would become magnets, places you said, *Yeah I want to go to* _____, *there's hella kids of color there.* Hella kids of color would be like three people, like Sunil, Kristen, and Rafael in Toronto, the mythical Pinay Latina mixed-kid happy rainbow alliance we heard tell was in the Bay, and all the alienated kids of color in Olympia who'd gone to Evergreen State because Riot Grrl and punk were political there and people talked about feelings and abuse and shit—all those folks who were now stuck there freaking the fuck out, surrounded by white kids and trees and banana slugs. We loved the punk rock and hated it and bitched constantly in our rooms about it and couldn't figure out how to go elsewhere, or where that elsewhere was. I'd had so many angst-ridden conversations in dorm rooms and crappy cheap bedrooms of messy apartments with The One Brown Kid, both of us shivering in our insecurity.

Except that we were figuring it out. Rafael started going to the Coalition Against Racist Police Violence meetings, where the whole thing was actually led by people of color, unlike ARA, which had had its moment of being made up mostly of dudes selling weed Rafael knew from selling weed around the Market but had inevitably been taken over by asinine white fourteen-year-old vegan children from the suburbs. Samira started tentatively going to Federation of Indian Leftists Meetings where everyone was forty or forty years older than her, anyways. They were all old-school desi communists who looked like our aunties but were flaming radicals who'd tried to make a revolution in Kerala, all tenderly happy to see that there was a new generation.

At *Prison News Service*, Anjali, Keisha, Rafael, and I decided that, in order to be on the collective, you had to be a person of color, poor, a psych survivor, or First Nations. We decided to carry out this directive by ceasing to call anyone we thought wasn't on the list to let them know when the meetings were. This hit a few snags, including, as I found out years later, Jordan, who was the most fucking annoying white girl in the scene. She was an aggressive hugger. She'd run up to you and try and throw her arms around you no matter what if you were a kid of color—you could be in the middle of a police riot outside the US consulate, and it wouldn't matter, she'd still try to hug you. One time, she tried to hug me when we were waiting for the bus to pull up outside the PIRG office to take us all to Philly for a Millions for Mumia protest, and my arms just automatically went into karate blocks to get hers from wrapping around me. I didn't mean them to; I just saw them floating up into the hexagonal blocks I'd learned at Brooklyn Women's Martial Arts and her face looking confused. It turned out that she'd grown up poor and been institutionalized as a kid, and she was really motherfucking pissed off at the fact we stopped calling her for the meetings. We just didn't know; I didn't know for years. Because, god knows you don't automatically feel all comfy saying you grew up living in a trailer in Kamloops, BC, and your folks had you locked up when you were a kid.

Despite the failures, we were a little cipher in the punk scene at the Markham Street house, and we were leaving it. Increasingly, it felt like staying in punk, getting into a huge fight at Who's Emma books over racism telling someone on the Riot Grrl listserv to stop saying that Latino men were soooo sexist wasn't just a pain in the ass, it was a waste of time. Why spend all that energy yelling at idiots? Why not just leave? There were all these people of color. Out there. Doing their own thing. Somewhere. We were the world majority, right? Out there. Not in tiny groups of two or three in the anarchist group, the activist meeting.

But, man, having Kristen, Rafael, and Sunil in that house felt like enough. Sure, Sunil had kind of an anger manage-ment problem, and Kristen would burst out crying when she was trying to type up the notes from the meeting and didn't really like other girls because they were "weak", but I'd take it. It just felt enough to be in the house with them for a minute. In January, Sunil would make beet curry and him and Rafael would eat it and then go to the cop shop and piss "fuck the police" in the snow in red piss so it looked like it was spelled out in blood. Kristen and us would all go to Pho Hung and order pho and split a large and pile on the free mint and chilies and bean sprouts. We would walk down the streets of Kensington looking for mangos in the garbage from the fruit stands, eating $2.99 breakfasts at The Greeks' diner, stamping off snow. And somehow, I wasn't afraid.

8. A Story of a River

No one's really sure where the Blackstone River is. It's a big dirty industrial river that's underground every single place it is, stuck in a culvert because it's too nasty to be aboveground. A lot of folks who live in Worcester don't know the river exists at all. But it's there.

It's a secret. Secret wild place that gave birth to this town. This dirty town is here because of the Blackstone River. It's where the Industrial Revolution was born. A lot of the earliest factories were built here. A lot of factories shut down. But the lead and asbestos and steel stays in the soil, and the water is fucked from all the chemicals. The reason why when I was growing up, my mama bought bottled water, even though she struggled over the food budget every week and shopped at Economy Fruit.

What there is in Worcester in the '80s and '90s is Dunkin' Donuts and empty red brick factory buildings, vacant lots and triple-deckers, a mall, working-class hair salons, Honey Farms mini-marts, and smoke shops. There was the abortion clinic, the old men's clothing shops; you don't know how they stay in business; Strawberries Records and the Nation of Islam guys who sold *The Final Call* on the Common, the welfare office downtown, along with a few used paperback stores, and a big old library at Salem Square. When stores or factories closed down, empty lots got taken over in a minute by thin weedy trees that busted through the concrete and made skinny, lush forests. Union Station was a big, beautiful, Greco-Roman monster building built back in the day when people took trains. It had been abandoned since the 1970s but if you snuck up to where it sits, where 280 meets 495 at the overpass, and got your eye close to a gap in the boards over the windows, you could see how maple seedling saplings shot through the floorboards. Under the marble high-domed ceilings and wrapped around the cracked novelties stand, there lived a secret forest.

No one was ever on the streets, and when they were, you had to worry. You also had to worry about the never-ending stream of assholes who hung out of their cars to yell shit at you and your ass. Sometimes they yelled, "Hey, chica!" at me, which confused me because though I wasn't supposed to be Puerto Rican, everybody thought I was anyway. I was somewhere in the beige brown shmear of light-brown/dark-brown hair, ethnic Massachusetts, Lebanese, Puerto Rican, light-skinned Black girl, or Greek.

My mother said that we were Caucasian. Indians were Caucasian. But we weren't Indian—we were from Ceylon. She'd say, "Your father's brown, your mother's white. When they ask, you should say you're beige."

When I asked my father what we were, he would bark, "Ceylonese" or "Burgher, we are Dutch Burgher," and storm out of the living room.

Then there was the time he was filling out census forms and

squinting at the box that said "Asian" and the subcategory that said "Other Asian" where there was a line where he could fill in something. It was 1990. I was fourteen.

I asked, "So, what are we, Dad?" and he barked, "Tamil!"

It wasn't a word I'd heard before, but it sounded familiar and ancient at the same time.

My father threw the papers down and stormed out of the room. He looked like his face was breaking with stories and silence and grief. And I was left to stare at those papers with their boxes that said, Check one: Caucasian Black Asian Latino (white) Other Latino Other Asian Native American.

Sometimes my dad would say he was Portuguese. That didn't really help in a state where Portuguese could check the "non-white" box on the census. Mostly, he changed the subject. Sometimes, when people asked my father where he was from after they squinted, he would say, "The British Commonwealth. Maybe you've heard of it? It used to own half the world."

My mother was fascinated by his family history and would tell us all kinds of stories. We had the photo albums that were the only two things that my grandparents had when they got on the last boat out of Malaysia when the Japanese invaded during World War II. My grandmother and grandfather, running with my dad, my grandmother pregnant with her second son, leaving behind a middle-class Sri Lankan house in Kuala Lumpur in the rain, with just two big leather photo albums.

Every morning, when my family stood hunched under the buzzing yellow fluorescent light by the factory-outlet kitchen table, drinking coffee as soon as it cleared the machine, my father looked stunned and pissed off, and one hundred percent as if he still wondered how the hell he ended up in Worcester in 1987. How did he end up in a two-storey colonial with a huge lawn to mow, water, and fertilize in a town without any good coffee anywhere, no servants, no warmth, no stink of Singapore smog or good tea from Malaya, now Malaysia, and, thank god, without his five-foot-two, medium-brown Ceylonese parents? How did he end up married to this small white woman he hadn't slept in the same bed with since the early '80s?

My mama raised me to hustle and she raised me to pass. She raised me to hate rich people, and she raised me to believe that if we made it, nothing would ever hurt again. She raised me on library books, factory-outlet shoes, factory-outlet everything, T.J. Maxx and Filene's Basement, Zayres, Caldor's, and Kmart (but not the Salvation Army—it wasn't cute to shop there; we were too close to poverty for it to not make us remember shame). My mama raised me to know that I was going to get the fuck out so I shouldn't love this place like I was going to stay. She raised me on stealing bricks from demolition sites in the middle of the night so we could make the front yard look like something from *Better Homes and Gardens*, except we didn't have any money to pay landscapers, it was just one working-class white woman polio survivor and one light brown twelve-year-old girl pouring cement and laying paving stones, prepped to tell the security guard, "Oh, the man told me I could have this for my herb garden" if we got stopped and to get away with it because she's a nice white lady. My mama raised me to have one accent for the oil company on the phone when the bill is late and one accent for us.

My mama raised me to know where I came from and love it and hate it. To always be ready for flight. To know that I wasn't like my cousins or the neighbors or anyone on the block because we read books, and she'd been to France. She raised me to believe that middle-class was both stupid and the beloved ground she hoped I'd land on someday, where I'd always have health insurance, no one would be hit, and people would talk about books and feelings. When I went away on scholarship to the teen art summer camp at Simon's Rock, an alternative college in western Massachusetts, all the kids were so mean because I didn't fit in. It was different than the young writer's conference I'd been to the previous year where I'd met all kinds of freaks who didn't hate me, most of whom I was still writing letters to. When I told her this, my mother said without pausing, "Well, Leah, it's a class thing. Those kids from the conference were, you know, regular. These kids are middle to upper middle-class. Of course they're more mean."

My mama raised me on the refrain of

You've got one ticket to ride, kid. Don't blow it.
Shit or get off the pot.
There ain't no such thing as a free lunch.

There were things I loved about Worcester. The library had every single book Marge Piercy had ever written, and I checked them out over and over again, because they were working-class feminist romance novels with politics and a plot, and when she talked about how much she loved Detroit, how green and wild it was, how skinny trees and pheasants take over every vacant lot in three weeks after it's abandoned, I thrilled in my toes. That's what it was like in Worcester—all fucked up with empty red brick warehouses, but some people take those over, rent them for super cheap, and make crazy installations, do things. Time's passed it by. Prices are from a decade ago. You can still rent a one bedroom for $350. It's not shiny, and you don't have to be either. There's so much potential. It's a place you can hide out in. You could make use of the warehouses and scrubby path woods they've ignored.

Worcester was the secret inside of the world. It was the beautiful in abandoned.

But as much as I'll always have this place imprinted on me, little bits of grit rubbed into my plush skin, as much as I see Pleasant Street, the Dunkin's on Chandler, the bookstore, and Institute Park on the inside of my eyelids all the time I am an adult, I was also poised to get out. I was always walking around with that hum in my hips, preparing for flight.

9. Survivor Psychic Powers

When I was a kid, I could always tell who were the survivor girls. It was a special talent. Some kids played tennis or were really good at video games. I could look at the kids in the hall between classes and could tell who was being molested.

Those girls, they fucked a lot behind the play structure or ate pencil shavings. They were crazy or were so good it made your teeth ache, or they set shit on fire or were always so ironed-down you just couldn't stand looking at them because you knew that someday, that girlbomb would just blow. They were the girls who floated out of their skin, just begging someone to fucking notice. I didn't know why I could see it. It hadn't happened to me, right?

In my family, my mother says, the women are psychic, just a little and just where it really counts. She was driving with my father and me one day when I was a baby; they were at a stop sign about to roll when she grabbed his arm for no reason and screamed, "*Justin!*" He was pissed, but right then, out of nowhere, a Cadillac barreled across the intersection and would have smashed their car to bits. Another time, she woke up out of a sound sleep, went downstairs without thinking about it, and saw that the pilot light had gone out and the kitchen was filling up with gas. I forget the third time. She says it's the ghost of her brother Johnny looking out for her, her favorite brother, the sweet one, not the drunk one, who made it home from Korea and got hit by a drunk driver and died a week later.

Her visions saved us. Me, I can see who's been abused, and I can see who's getting hit. I can tell who's puking in the girls' bathroom. I can see all this shit, but I can't do shit about it except wait.

But maybe incest was everywhere. In the tap water, in the air, in the mall. Every goddamn where. Every girl you knew. Maybe some of the boys too. What would that mean, if incest was everywhere? If every girl you knew told you shit in the basement of their house, whispering while you were watching *Children of the Corn* and eating Fritos, or if you knew by the way she turned her body in the locker room? But if you were their friend, you wouldn't tell anybody—not the school counselor or your mom. All you could do was hold the secret close.

What would it mean if it was everywhere, the secret that was that close?

10. Gasoline in the Eyes

There's some moments in the life of a survivor girl that stand out.

Like the day you get your full height, finally, and you might still be twelve years old, but things shift. Maybe you stop crying all the time when you get yelled at. Maybe the rage of the girl inside you, maybe it starts staring out your eyes at your parent. Maybe your parent starts being a little afraid of you.

Like a lot of femmes of color, I got my height, weight, tits, hips, and blood early. Suzy Abadi, the other brown girl, and I got our tits and armpit hair in fifth grade. I was five-foot-six by seventh grade and had been bleeding for a year. I used to wear those Always Super night pads with wings to school because I was paranoid that if I went to the bathroom a lot people would figure out I was bleeding and have something else to fuck with me for.

Five-foot-six, and then I stopped growing. I'd always been one of the tallest, one of the leanest girls in class. My dad was six-foot-three. My mom was five-foot-three. People said I took after my dad. I looked like my dad. I would smirk when people said that and then think, *I may look like my dad, but inside, I'm all like my mom.* Five-six, small tits, long legs, long brown curly hair to my butt and an ass. One of those girls who is fourteen but looks twenty-five.

My dad learned how to drive a week before my mother went into labor, and he never became a good driver. He drove with all the muffled fury he felt about his whole entire life. He'd go eighty miles an hour on a two-lane road, passing every driver, muttering SHITSHITSHIT between his teeth. The car would get real quiet and fill with the aroma of all of our sweat and fear and everything we never said out loud as a family. I would ask him to go slower, he would bark at me, my mother would cry, and I would cry. My mom was a great driver, always had been, but when she picked him up from work, she would slide over and give him the wheel. Maybe it's what she thought she was supposed to do. Maybe she was tired of driving all the time everywhere, doing everything. Maybe both.

In *Woman on the Edge of Time*, every kid has three mothers, and Marge Piercy explained that no one really needs a dad— what you need is mothering, loving, comfort, holding. I agreed entirely. My memories of my dad are of him being gone, or of him being on fire.

But then there's this memory of me at the age of twelve. It's a Saturday morning in May or June. My father had to mow the lawn, our big-ass lawn. He hated it. He hated most of his life. He was screaming, "Shit!" so loud that everybody on the block could hear him. Like the way he screamed SHITMOTHERFUCK-ERJESUSCHRISTSONOFAFUCKINGBITCHBUGGER every time he drove eighty-five miles an hour as my mother silently cried and said, "Justin, can you please slow down." Like all the reasons why I hated him. Like why I decided not to go to Australia for Christmas with him in 1986—the one chance I had to meet my Sri Lankan grandparents—because I couldn't cope with the thought of being with him in airports for twenty-four hours. I wanted the kind of Christmas you have when the abusive parent leaves.

I remember being a long-legged twelve-year-old girl child standing in front of him as he squatted, swearing and cursing at the lawnmower. I don't remember my arm moving. But I remember, oh, I remember, taking the gas can and throwing the gasoline in his eyes. I remember him screaming. I remember not being there.

I remember my mother driving my father to the hospital. I didn't go with them. I went to my bedroom, sat crossed-legged quiet on the twin bed, and wondered what would happen. When they got home hours later, my mother told me that my father's eyes had had to be washed by a machine for several hours to get the gas out.

But I don't remember being punished.

My father started to look differently at me, with a look I hadn't seen before. He'd started looking afraid of me. And like he wasn't sure what to do about it.

Maybe I would steal his car. Blow up his house. Burn it down. Who knows what I would do.

Part 2

GOING INTO THE SKY

11. The Last Time I Went Home for Christmas

The last time I went home for Christmas, my mom cut off all my hair.

I had head lice. Maybe they'd jumped from someone else's head to my head in the subway. More likely they came from a hat that I'd grabbed from the free box in the front hallway of the Toronto ARA house and had worn without washing. I don't know how I got them.

I was in my parents' shower after Christmas-present opening.

I was twenty-one years old. Which is the age of some of the youth I work with and love, and now that I am no longer twenty-one, I can see just how young and old they are. At the time, I didn't know how to feel my youth or my age. I was a crazy girl-bomb old young woman, but no way in hell was I young in any way that meant vulnerable.

I was in the shower. Black and white tile. Head itching like crazy. I scratched the dandruff out from my head with my nails and wiped it on the bathroom tile. I know this is gross. When I looked at it a few moments later, I saw things in it. Little black dots. Some of them were moving. I stared at them from a while, then screamed for my mother. I think.

There is a blank where I say something, where I call for her, where she comes. Then there is her shoving my head in the sink, the same way she did when I was six or seven years old when she washed my hair in the sink, and I would run from her screaming like I was possessed, like I was running from her for my fucking life. Like I am a kid who doesn't want her hair washed, who screams because it's what kids do.

My mother gets a pair of scissors.

My mom cuts all my hair off. Almost all of it.

....

Story Version One

There was nothing else to do; I had dreadlocks, and I had head lice. I hated those dreads anyway; getting them had been a huge embarrassing mistake. I had been hedging for a year and a half over what to do with them because I knew that once I chopped them off I would have almost no hair, and it would take a couple of years to grow back. I said yes when my mother, who definitely had not been counting on this as her Christmas afternoon activity, suggested cutting my hair off to get rid of the lice. I muttered and said, *Fuck it, there's nothing for it but to cut them off.* Why did I have dreadlocks? Yeah, good question.

I had dreads because I had done double-dip mescaline with an erstwhile boyfriend on New Year's Eve 1994.

I had done double-dip mescaline even though I'd just

recently stopped feeling very crazy all of the time, and hallucinogenic drugs probably weren't the smartest idea. But I wanted to be nineteen—normal, doing drugs and not crazy.

I had had some visions. Had been just kind of normal stoned for a while, but then I'd smoked a bowl and drank a forty of Old English, and my ego had died along with my ability to use verbal language. I had ended up with my dumb blond boyfriend in his car in the parking lot of a Dunkin' Donuts somewhere near Billerica, MA, that faced onto a nature preserve. My hallucinations had gotten more vivid, including one of little broken baby dolls appearing in the trees. The limbs of the trees turned into the broken-off legs of little girl ballerinas. At five a.m., we had driven home to his parents' house where I had passed out on the couch in the living room, and where his mother kept her cuckoo clock collection. I lay there, coming down from my high, watching the sun come up, hearing all her clocks go off every hour. She didn't have them timed to each other. I snuck out, got the bus to Cambridge, and sat there on a bench, smoking my smokes and drinking my coffee: Everything was washed clean. My brain was fresh. I loved drugs.

After I made it home to New York, to my empty apartment, I had decided that I had to Do It. To Live For Real and Be Really Real and Face My Fears.

So I locked my hair.

I had been staring at photos of sadhus, holy men, in South India and Sri Lanka. They let those big, Dravidian curls lock.

I lived in a Puerto Rican and white squatter neighborhood,

full of Puerto Rican and white and some Black squatters with dreads. It was a mark of your resistance. You didn't pay rent, and you locked your hair.

I didn't know what to do with my hair, and

I didn't know who or how to ask.

It felt like the Lower East Side was just going to break off

like there was a line down First Avenue

and we would be able to secede

for real.

I felt bad about paying $300 rent. Rent was theft, and there were so many leaning, liberated palaces throughout the neighborhood that were excellent sources of free housing.

I was supposed to drop out of college and stop paying rent and make it happen.

Except that my mother had just about killed herself working two, three jobs, saving, scrimping, never giving herself shit so that I could go to college, real college.

I was a working-class girl, a first-generation college student who already had bumped into the racismsexismclassismhomophobiajeeeeeeezus of the Lower East Side majority white dude activist scene.

It felt like a showdown. One of many. Between what I was supposed to do and what felt right, what felt like what my soul wanted. And my knowledge that I was not some trust fund kid with college waiting. This was my one ticket to ride. My mom had saved up money to give me that Mac Classic. If I moved into the squat and someone ripped that shit off, there would not be another one waiting.

So in that moment, although I thought I would drop out of school too, I started by dreading my hair.

I did not know what I was motherfucking doing.

What I did do was snip off sections of the stereo wire in my closet, left over from when I'd bought my turntable (bought so that I could listen to vinyl, like any good punk trying to keep it real in 1994. CDs were evil. I'd felt guilty buying Hole's *Miss World* album from Tower Records on cassette. Everything was supposed to be purchased from ABC No Rio, the art and activism center in the Lower East Side, or by mail-order distros in the back of *Maximum Rocknroll* or a zine). I snipped off sections of copper and silver wire and sectioned off my hair, rubbed in some Let's Dread from Ricky's midnight drugstore, and waited.

It was obvious really fast that the whole thing was a terrible ugly mistake. I got thick chunky dreads with lumps in them. Not dreads, matts. The kind non-Black hair makes,I don't care about that shit that all you need is one African ancestor give you permission to dread, and that includes going-back-to-the-dawn-of-the-human-species-since-we-all-came-from-Africa shit. No one who is not Black gets to "dread" their hair. Those are the rules of what is right. In 1995, I hadn't yet read any of the articles about cultural appropriation and anti Black racism and how white and POC's trying to "dread" their hair was wrong, but I had common sense. The common sense that kicked in right after I did it, where I stared in the mirror and thought, I never should have done this, nobody who isn't Black should do this. I had pulled out all the hair I could. Which meant that I had a layer of curls on the top and then a couple, okay, more than a couple, of very thick rod-like dreads that I tried to hide as best I could underneath the curls. I was trying to deal with it later. It wasn't that obvious unless I tried to put my hair up.

This is why I did it: the conflux of sadhus, the Lower East Side, and one brown crazy mesc-soaked nineteen-year-old girl with a complex.

But that Christmas, I curled up amid pale blue walls in the twin bed that made me feel slightly sick, a chair pushed against the door, waiting for my mother to call for me, to ask where I am, what I am doing. I cry like my heart is broken and count the days til I can go back to New York on the bus, to smoke, mangoes, fried plantain, and being safe. I am not crying about losing those mats of hair. I'm crying about my mom cutting all my hair off and calling me filthy.

....

Story Version Two

My mother shoves my head down in the sink like she did when I was a little kid fighting having my hair washed, like how she brushed my hair straight under the blow dryer every morning for years til my scalp ached raw, it always felt fucked-up, she always felt angry to me when she was doing it. My white mama is shoving my head down under running water and all I can feel is *can't breathe choking* underwater, is her cutting all my hair off is her telling me how dirty I am how dirty my hair is how dirty I am, her tone is grim and disgusted by my curly hair my filth the filth I got from hanging out with dirty people the confluence with Blackness the rage she feels at her life at my life at me not turning out the way the plan was supposed to go.

She shoves my head down that wet white hole, and I'm tiny, a pinpoint, disappeared and also huge and blackpurplesnarl, remembering shit in my body. It's too much, and it's in the list of shit that's forbidden to ever mention feeling; it's crazy, it's locked up, it's before and after words. You don't say it. And when I stand up, I have lost ninety percent of my hair.

My mother takes my hair and throws it deep in a snowbank out back. After dinner, after she has furiously put all the clothes and bed linens through an extra-hot wash with bleach, when she is in bed, I open the screen door slowly and tiptoe out to where I see the bag and pull just a few of those locks out.

and we never speak of it
and I don't even let myself feel how fucked-up I look and
feel—my hair is gone.
it grows back slowly
a couple years slowly
this is the next-to-last time I'm here.

....

Backstory

I didn't know I had curly hair til I was eleven or twelve.

I didn't know that because I wasn't allowed to wash my hair

and do it til then.

Is that normal?

Is it normal that I wasn't allowed to close my door all the way?

That I remember it taking a protracted battle that caused her to cry a lot, to win that right in my twenties?

Or was what happened that I was afraid of the dark for a really long time, so I was the one who left the door open?

Or are they both true?

Is it normal that my mom would come in and knock on my door "just checking" every hour or so?

Is it normal that she would stop talking to us for a couple of days sometimes?

I didn't know I had curly hair
and my curly hair was always a mark of something wild and
    dark and out of control and dirty and painful and hard
    to clean or make look beautiful.
When I grow up
I will always have
long
beautiful
lots of
curly
curly
brown and pink hair.

12. Mom

Mom. Not monster. Just mom. Much better than her mom. Still did some things wrong.

Your mom brushes your hair straight when you're a kid. She sits you down in front of her vanity with the curvy brown wood on either side of the mirror, the tabletop with its bottle of Chanel No. Five (which she measures out, one drop behind each ear each day, making it last), her Cover Girl powder-blue eyeshadow, her Mason Pearson hairbrush. It is black, from London where she met Dad, with a bright orangey-red back and sharp black bristles. Your hair is so thick, tangled, troublesome. She brushes, and you squirm and ouch. And when she is done, it is worse; somehow, your hair does not calm down the way it should but gets bigger and frizzier around your face, a vast wilderness of bushy brown frizz. You hate it, but you go to school anyway.

Until you were seven or eight, it was wavy, not curly, and you wore it with bangs and those '70s woven ribbon barrettes. In the '70s, it felt like things were getting better. Okay, you were four, but it still felt that way. There was Jimmy Carter. In the '80s, it felt like it was getting worse. There was Reagan, the mean kids at the new private school you were at on scholarship, ugly fashions, and your hair and legs rebelling, getting darker, thicker.

Back to your mom: she brushed your hair hard. Sometimes she brushed and blow-dried your hair at the same time. It took forty-five minutes. Sometimes it felt like your scalp was bleeding. You twisted and turned. It felt wrong, but that was a sign that you were wrong.

You didn't really know you had curly hair til you were twelve, when she finally, reluctantly, let you take over the work yourself. You shampooed your hair and conditioned it, using the tons of conditioner you needed to comb it through. You cautiously bought one of the picks that Black people use from the drugstore, and you used this to comb out your hair when you got out of the shower. It was hot that day, so you let it air dry. It dried into ... curls. Big ones, You stared at your face.

In seventh grade, you are a feminist, small-press nerd, so you have been reading things, pretty much anything in the 340 section of the library. You read things and then you read the bibliography and suggested other readings in the back; you write down the titles and look them up in the card catalog. You have heard of a book called *This Bridge Called My Back* that people keep mentioning, but it is not in the Worcester Public Library. You find it on one of your monthly trips to Cambridge, and you take it to your mother, saying this is the book you want to buy. You can spend twenty dollars on each visit. She squints at this book and looks at you, and you are afraid, afraid that she is going to say no. She never does; she says that she wants you to read and read and read. She squints at you over the book, and you can't tell if she's afraid and angry or is about to lose it the way she does sometimes. You don't know why she would be angry, but you sense she might be. And she buys it for you anyway.

You don't get why you like that book more than other books you read. You can relate to it more than anything else you've read, but that's wrong. The women in the book are that term, "women of color." You must be faking—what is that? You are just normal. And weird. You stare at yourself in the mirror, though. Thick-ass winging eyebrows, light brown skin (no lighter than some of the Puerto Rican girls, or the Armenians or Lebanese, but they're white too, right?) Lebanese is almost Greek in this town, it's like Armenian. That thick curly hair that's also in your armpits and legs. Woman of color. Are you? Can you say it? You are a girl, even though you look twenty-five. In your head, you are twenty-five too.

When you are a kid, you think Cambridge is heaven. There are bookstores, like maybe forty of them, and there are people walking around on the streets til late, but not the kind of people you have to be scared of. You don't feel scared. There is never enough time for you to spend in the aisles of Wordsworth or the poetry bookstore, never enough time to eat good pizza, follow your father to the comic book store. Your mother keeps telling you that this is where the smart people are. This is where you will go to college, and this is why it doesn't matter that you don't have friends, because when you get a scholarship to go to college here, you will meet them. And then she flashes back to her grad school days in London, sitting at a long table with your father and all the others, eating cheap spaghetti and cheap red wine, laughing. She was so happy then. Sometimes you think it was the last time she was really happy.

You live on a dead-end street because it is supposed to be safer, and you are not allowed to walk off the end of it, even though you live in a quiet, residential block in the second-best zip code of Worcester, Mass, which is not saying a whole lot. When you spend too long in the backyard or off the street, your mom yells for you, and there is a level of panic in her voice that seems extra to what your friends or the kids you know hear. She tells you if you go off the street you will be raped.

You mom is a frail-looking woman, small but tough. She walks with a slowness, a pain she won't mention but is always there. She had polio as a kid. The story is that her parents didn't have enough money to see a doctor more than once, but the doctor they took her to told them to buy her a bicycle. "With any luck, she'll ride it out." She did. Well enough. I realized, much later, that if she had to walk more than 100 yards, she slowed, and her hip canted up and her whole body hurt. She would never call herself disabled. Working-class women suck it up.

Your mother works and works. She works teaching, even in Worcester, where there has been a hiring freeze on teachers since the early '80s. At night, she lies in her recliner in the sunroom and works more, for extra money, correcting papers and curriculum and lesson plans for mail-order correspondence courses from the American Management Association.

Your mother handles everything. She gets up on a ladder and cleans out the gutters of the house and garage. She takes her paychecks, and she takes your dad's paycheck. She takes all the bills, and she pays them. She gives your dad an allowance.

She takes you with her in the gray Volvo to do errands, and you zone out in the passenger seat with your library books. You usually grab a serious stack of books to go anywhere. When you are twenty-one, she will pull over by the bank parking lot, cut off the engine, and say, "Leah, I have something to tell you. There's an account in here that your father doesn't know anything about. I've been taking money from his paychecks, well, when he had one. There's $10,000 in there. I'm going to put your name on it, and if anything happens to me, it's all yours."

She says things to you like, "Leah, in a marriage, there is always one person who has the upper hand. Make sure it's you," and "Don't marry someone stupider than you like I did."

She calls your dad "the houseboy" and "the idiot" and laughs.

Your mom, you love her more than your dad. She is there for you, day after day after day. Anyone who knows you—to the degree that she lets people know you and her—can see that you love each other so much and are so tight, tighter than any other mother and daughter of all time. She is not constantly angry the way your dad is. She makes sense. Tells you about working-class history. Tells you repeatedly, til she is past the point of exhaustion, that it is okay to be weird, to be different, that when you go away to college it is going to be okay, that you will go to college.

Your mom, you love her more than your dad. How can you not? She loves you, feeds you, and buys you discount clothes at

Filene's Basement. Except that, there are times you can't really let yourself think about, when she fades away. The times she says, "I don't have to hit you like my parents did me. I just stop loving you for a few days and you fall right in line." The times she grabs your butt, the times she will not talk to you for a few days, the times she runs up the stairs and throws herself on the king-sized bed, sobbing. You will fear exposure if you show these things to the world. You are the world's worst daughter, most ungrateful daughter. She gave up her whole life to send you to college.

Your mother wanted you to go to college with a will of iron and a single-minded focus that was like a steel bar in her shoulders, that showed in her furrowed forehead, squinting over all those grade-seven papers on noun clauses and mail-order correspondence business courses. She pushed you like working-class and immigrant mothers do. Your mother says things like, "You can have friends when you go to college." You are in public grade school through grade two, but she doesn't let you get any books except those from the advanced-reader section in the weekly book club, and frowns like she wants to hit you when you ask if you can buy *Curious George*. When Massachusetts has a taxpayer's revolt in 1982 and votes overwhelmingly to slash property taxes, decimates the public school system in 1982, killing the art, music, gifted, and sports programs over-night, and fires all the teachers under the age of fifty, she has you in the admissions office of Bancroft, a local private K–12 day school, the next day. You perform exceptionality there, and you get admitted on financial aid. You get your ass kicked by the rich white kids at Bancroft every day and start to feel a chronic, suicidal depression that will stick around for a long time. But you do love the small classes, books, and the teachers who love you because you are reading ahead of grade-level already. Your mother's will to get you into college pushes you into all the extracurricular activities you can get, AP classes and special prep time for them on the weekends; pushes you to memorize all the crap so you can maintain straight As, so that you can get the fattest scholarship package to the best college you can. It means ten years of being in a school where you will get your ass beat, where boys will chase you around with supersoakers filled with orange Kool Aid, squirting your clothes, where all the seventh-grade boys chase you from the science building to Ms. Howe's English class across campus trying to pin you down to feel your breasts and throw rocks at your head when they can't. You will hate it and long for friends and peace and the ability to wear jeans, but when you get the University Scholars scholarship to NYU with its two free trips a year, one domestic and one international, you will take it and run, run, run.

You hesitate to write about your mother all these years later. You don't want to be Rebecca Walker, talking shit about her mom morning, noon, and night in her memoirs. Years after all your early-twenties rage, you will have compassion for your mother. You will be able to hold in your mind all the ways you loved her, the ways you still love and respect her and are thankful for her heroism and courage. You can say: This is not a story about hating the abuser, about the abuser as monster. Some abusers are monsters, but most are not. If they were nothing but horrible looming giants who tore through our days, even the neck-high levels of denial and dissociation in this culture would not allow the abuse perpetuated to stand.

Your mother is someone who touched you in ways she shouldn't, was angry in ways she shouldn't have been, who didn't let you walk off the block or close your door. She was the white mom who brushed your scalp straight til it bled and who cried when you called yourself a woman of color. She is the fingers in your baby genitals that ripped your mind, made you leave your body early. She is the hole in your hips, the core of the hurricane that would mess up your life and make you crazy, in ragged pieces, for years and years, under all your carefully groomed, holding-it-together, straight-A face. She is the woman whose love was enough to let you live to grow up, to get out.

You will walk out of her house and her life, you will not speak for years. You will regrow yourself. You will get sick like she is sick, but you will also walk out of her burning house, her closed-up cold house. Your house's doors are open and closed, and your whole life is that grad-student table spilling cheap food and friends. You have therapy, orgasms, your own bank account, your own house, an art career, love, and a thousand friends to catch you when you fall.

In your heart, you sing as much as you cry: this life is what she wanted for you, her dearest hope.

She is not a monster. She is your mother. The mother who abused you. The mother who loved you.

Your mother taught you to dig things up. You will use the tools she gave you. Just on your family. On yourself.

13. A Good Brother

It was a few months after I'd moved in with Rafael.

Some nights I'd be grabbing his legs and pulling him back as he tried to fit himself through the fifth-storey window. Some days I'd run after him and jam my shoulder into the door he was trying to close as he howled that he was going to cut his throat. Sometimes he'd wrap the curtains around his neck and try to choke himself.

Nobody at the meetings saw or heard anything about this.

According to the copy of *Allies in Healing* stashed in the line of milk-crate bookcases along the long south wall of our one-room apartment (getting more dog-eared every day), confidentiality in survivor-survivor relationships means that if one person doesn't want you to talk about it, then you don't. So I didn't. Tell anyone anything.

"Everyone in the community still thinks I'm crazy," Rafael would say, ranting and sipping on a double-double crap coffee and sometimes smoking a loosie. "They're prejudiced against psych survivors, and I didn't exactly have the best reputation when I came back from Vancouver. If you say anything to anyone, it'll just destroy me."

I'd nod. So I didn't, and meetings were a break from fighting. There was the one night, though. The Gravediggaz were blasting at volume twelve on the boom box.

The phone rang. It was my friend Anna.

"Um, hi?" she said. She could probably hear the music blasting.

I tried not to sound like I was crying. "What's up with you?"

"Superdiva? Are you okay?"

"Um, yeah, everything's cool. Can I call you back? This isn't a good time."

"What the fuck do you mean, 'It's not a good time?' Don't say that! She'll know something's wrong!" Rafael screamed from the bathroom.

"Uh, yeah, gotta go."

"Okay, call me later, okay?" I hung up without saying anything. That night, the cops finally showed up. Maybe she called him, maybe the neighbors did. There was that safety plan we'd made out of the *Men Who Hurt the People Who Love Them* book we'd mail-ordered, the one that was the sole resource in the Violent People Who Want To Change section at the back of *The Courage to Heal*. The strategy was that, if things got bad, I would go out for a walk until things calmed down. Things were going bad.

"Um, I think I'm going to the Coffee Time for a while," I said, trying to sound calm and matter-of-fact.

"Like hell you are."

There were some serious problems with the safety plan, like why was I supposed to leave when I was not the one going crazy and banging my head into the wall? How was I supposed to know when things had calmed down?

"Rafael, I'm just doing what was in the safety plan."

"You're not fucking going anywhere."

Something rose up inside me like your gorge before you vomit. "Yeah, I am." I got up. Rafael jumped so fast in front of me and blocked the doorway that I didn't even see how he got there. I tried to reach past, and he blocked me. Reached past again—the same thing. There was a shitty little closet next to the door with thin plastic sliding doors that held the can of gasoline for setting fire to shit, spray paint from painting *Pepita y Chanchito '97* under the underpass, extra bags of clothes and books, and I snorted up the snot and turned and went and sat in it, curled up over my legs.

"What the fuck do you think you're doing?" Rafael started to kick the thin doors with his boots, pounding the thin plastic. Thunk. "Stop!" Thunk. "Stop!" Thunk.

The whole closet was shaking.

Holy fucking shit, what if it breaks?

When that stuff happened, I got small. It was like my body was on the static channel on the TV that comes on after the programs were gone. Every hair on my body stood up, but my brain was blank, someplace else, humming. Change the channel til this program's over.

And then the door buzzer farted an angry BAARRRRRR.

Rafael ran into the john, saying, "I'm not here."

I climbed out of the closet, shaking. Walked the one step to the door. My legs didn't feel like they could go much farther.

"Hello?"

"This is the police. We've gotten a complaint about a disturbance in your apartment."

"Um, what?" I could see Rafael in his shorts, no shirt, creeping out of the bathroom. He ran a finger across his throat.

"A disturbance, ma'am."

"Uh, I don't know what that could've been. We were playing some music. Maybe that was it." I was trying my best to sound normal, but I could tell I wasn't pulling it off.

"It didn't sound like music, ma'am."

"Um, well, I'm not sure what that could've been." It was like the ghost of me at the border. A lot fainter.

I could hear one cop mutter to another, "She won't open the door." Then even louder banging, slam slam slam, like they were trying to break it down.

"Okay, okay, I'll open it."

I opened the door. There was an older white cop with a spare tire and bags under his eyes, and his younger, browner partner. They stood there smirking at our sorry apartment. Rafael came out of the john and said hi. He was shooting me the *Don't rat me out look* from his eyes, trying to be subtle, as if the cops could miss anything in our 150 square feet. The white guy stayed quiet as the younger, brasher brown one ran our IDs. I knew from the pamphlets at the legal clinic and what the hotline counselor had told me on the phone that they had to do a mandatory arrest if they were called in for partner abuse. The browner one looked up. "So you're on probation, huh?"

"Yeah," said Rafael.

"For what? Assault, huh? That's nice, that's real nice." *Oh please oh please don't have the record say anything about how it was assault police, even though it'd been three cops who beat the shit out of him. Please.*

"Looks like you have a couple of assaults under your belt. How'd you like me to run you in?"

They weren't looking at me.

We can kill you. We can make it look like an accident. No one would know. No one would even care. I stepped forward a half step. "Please. Nothing happened. We were fighting, but nothing physical happened. Really. There's a lot of crazy people in this building."

He stared at me for a long time, then snapped his notebook shut. "Fine. We better not hear anything from this apartment again."

"See ya, scum!" the other guy yelled as they clomped out in their heavy cop boots. Rafael didn't say anything. I curled up like a pinworm on the twin futon and tried to will myself to sleep. Rafael turned the Gravediggaz off.

Another night I made it out of the house, backing away, saying I was going to the Coffee Time—I walked out, past the security guards, past the guys hanging outside the door.

I walked past the groups of guys outside every bar and all-night, old-man's espresso bars as the streets gradually got less war zone. Dufferin, Ossington, Christie, Bathurst. Counting the streets and blocks, noting them. Thinking very steadily about the sociological aspects of those streets and nothing else. Except: calm, quiet, alone. Walking steady, dodging the *hey baby*s and *c'mere*s.

I was a few blocks beyond Bathurst in the Annex, walking

past bookstores and falafel places and coffee shops, steady, head down. I wasn't sure where I was going, I was just walking. A car of frat boys was driving by. One of them stuck his head out of the window.

"Oh my god." He sounded matter of fact, almost tender at first.

"You are so ugly. You're the ugliest girl I've ever seen." The window slammed up, and the car sped off.

I turned down the next street that led to an alleyway after that. Toronto had good alleys. Despite what you picture, I had never found any good ones in New York. Toronto's were nice and big, with good graffiti on the roll-down doors of garages. They had edible weeds, stands of lambs quarters or plantain that I could stop to munch on. Sometimes mulberries or blackberries. There were flowers in the Annex homeowners' nice native perennial gardens. I made a left, then a right, got down to College, and had to figure out what to do, how many more steps this walk could hold.

I always eventually went home. Where else could I go? Rafael would be asleep or sitting up waiting for me. We'd talk about something neutral. Go to bed.

We found a new place to live. I was convinced that, if we moved out of the building, with its cop-calling neighbors and security guards, if we could be some place with a backyard, some place less crazy and more private, everything would be better. I wouldn't be trying to take space by reading on the toilet with the door closed on our one room. We'd have the healing power of the earth. Or something.

Somebody Rafael knew at CKLN knew about the house on Dupont. It was one block over from our building, but it had a backyard and a living room, a bedroom, a kitchen. As soon as I saw it, I thought, *Yes*, and then, *everything will be okay here*. It was just a fucked-up house smack in the middle of nowhere, right behind the railroad tracks and sandwiched in between a cement company and an auto repair place. The CN high-power line was right behind the tracks, and there was a tiny little ho stroll past the auto repair, by some abandoned Portuguese social club. But it was a house. It had a backyard to dump my buckets of menstrual blood in and a fence with wild grapes growing on it that I could hang a clothesline from. It was perfect. A house in a narrow strip of six semi-detached houses that were all kind of leaning and fucked-up in the middle of a mini-zone of industrial waste. There were two rooms with doors that shut, windows that looked out onto trees and railroad, and a big white bathroom with a big white bathtub and built-in shelves and moldings.

We moved the whole way in shopping carts, from one block to another, which gave a certain panache to the whole thing, especially when the cops rolled by as Rafael was pushing the big old TV we'd inherited from one of his uncles. They slowed down and crept by us as we kept looking straight ahead, not provoking, grinding our teeth, pushing all our shit past the gas station.

14. June 17, 1997

Running.

The streetlights pooled yellow and black on Dupont.
My knee ground into the busted-up concrete,
the sightline of the old cabinet factory at the corner of
    Bartlett,
and his knee in my back,
and the sound of him sobbing.

"Hey, don't do that to your fucking woman, man!" A bunch of
frat boys in an Impala leaning out as they screeched by.
His knee in my back.

"Pepita, pepita!" Muffled sobbing. "I'm sorry! I'm so fucking
sorry!"

Rain dripping.
"Hey, I, uh, I gotta go—"
"No! No! Don't leave me! You know I'm gonna kill myself if you
leave!"

"It's okay, man. I'm gonna just go. I'm gonna. Just. Go. Like, by myself for an hour. And then I'll come back. Okay?"

The cabinet factory, the corner of Dupont and Bartlett with its six little houses, all peach vinyl siding and two-foot-wide, no-grass front yards, huddled in the middle of the sheet metal, industrial nursery, and gravel places, toes kissing the railroad tracks. Mr Vu's perennial yard sale and the Portuguese community hall. It was dark, and the two blocks before Dufferin were a ho stroll sometimes, but that night it was just dark and empty of girls as I walked away, that garish pink and lime-green Guatemalan hippie backpack over my arms, over the garish '70s blue and hot-pink polyester paisley skirt I'd been wearing when it all went down. Skinny strap black tank top. A fucked-up left knee with gravel ground into it, with a big scab forming, the kind that's gonna be thick like cardboard. Not looking back. Through the dark to the bus stop at Dufferin, lit up by the drive-through McDonalds, the smell of the closed roses stand. The bus stop. Take it. Go to Anna's house. Go.

I was flat as paper, only I remember that I was sobbing, that my chest was shaking. My eyeliner was running all over my face. I was trying to pull it together, to pass, so no one would mess with me, no one would mess me up, the cops wouldn't see a sobbing female at the Dufferin bus stop and stop. I don't know if I had any money. My ATM card wouldn't help me get on the bus. The bus rolled up.

I got on. The lady bus driver had weary rocker eyeliner, big bags under her eyes, and some lank layers growing out.

"Hi," I said. "Um. My boyfriend just hit me. I don't have any change, but I really need to be on this bus."

She barely glanced at me. Laid on the horn, moved the wheel, kicked the bus out of its stop. Kept her eyes straight ahead. "Where are you going?"

"To a friend's place."

She didn't nod her head or say anything or look at me, just kept driving, but she didn't say "No, get off," either. So I walked to the back of the bus, sat down, and tried to wipe off the drooling eyeliner, stop my chest from heaving. Tried to fold my face up like paper; it was a letter no one could read. The passengers all looked away, their faces folded flat.

Anna's place. A big industrial loft. A little kitchen tucked warmly in the corner with forty-pound bags of Mr. Gouda's dhal, black-eyed peas, rice, and small bags of West Indian curry powder in the cupboard. When she got a good job, the first thing she did was go out and buy huge sacks of dry goods so that, if she lost her job again, she'd have food. She called me Superdiva and chuckled and smiled at me as she fixed bikes in the big vise in the corner. "Does this seem like the kind of place that yuppies would live in?" Anna would ask, and I'd shake my head no. It was kind of true; her place was nicer than anyone else's I knew, but even if it did look like one of those anathema yuppie live-work spaces, I loved the wood floors and the way the light fell on them. I was on my way to Anna's.

An hour ago, it had been like this: We were in the apartment. He was pacing. I was tensing up. We were fighting over something like the color we should paint the living room—it didn't matter. The tension was rising again. I got up and started to go, for the millionth time. Rafael said, menace in his voice, "Oh no, you're not. You're not fucking going anywhere." He stared me down. Like that was just a fact.

Inside me, there was this little heart-break silent squash every time that happened. I'd think, *Remember, remember the safety plan we made? From the* For Men Who Hurt The Women Who Love Them *workbook we special-ordered from the Women's Bookstore?* When we sensed that the tension-building phase of the cycle of violence was on its way, Rafael was supposed to refer to a list of things he should do to calm his ass down, like drinking tea or calling one of the folks whose name was on a list thumbtacked to the wall. If that didn't work, he was supposed to leave. I think so; that would have been the right thing, but maybe it was just straight to step three: She Leaves. Like I had before. I was going, *Wait, this is what we said, he agreed, I don't understand, fuck this.*

I stood up. Brittle, but somewhere inside me there was a sassy, *Bitch, don't fuck with me* thing. "Oh, no, I'm leaving." I walked down the hallway. I got to the top of the stairs.

Then, his arm around my body, that pint-sized wrestler's build, his hands around my neck. "I said you're not fucking going anywhere."

At Brooklyn Women's Martial Arts, they'd said, "We train you hard, make you drill over and over again, so that if anything happens, you won't have to think; your body will just react."

My body reacted. My arms went up inside his elbows, in the move they called the Volcano. The elbows are a weak point; it doesn't matter how big the man—hell, anybody—is, the elbows are weak. Any joint, anything that bends and folds is weak. His arms grabbed for me. I flew across the plastic carpet runner, flew down the stairs. I got three feet.

Whenever some crazy shit happened I went to that place. I wasn't disassociated, didn't make my eyeballs blur, my head up in the trees to one branch all gold. But I went someplace like inky blue night, skinny like paper, where it was cold. Doing what I needed to do and stayed psychic enough to figure out who I needed to be and become that person, to slip through.

Off the bus. College and Dufferin, Starbank convenience store. Trotting. *How long til he realizes I'm not coming back?*

I hit Anna's buzzer. Anna wasn't answering her buzzer or her phone. But often she didn't. She mostly screened calls, letting the voicemail pick them up. No one had call-display back then, and any call could have been her crazy dad or somebody else she didn't feel like talking to. She was the one who'd introduced me to the concept of not picking up the phone, ever, just listening to the messages and getting back to people when you felt like it. I mean, I had done that before too, but it was more guilt-ridden flakiness than a conscious choice. Was that what she was doing right now? "Anna," I said. "Pick up, for real. Rafael hit me, and I'm at the payphone at the convenience store across the street."

Anna and her warm room. She'd put some dub cassette on the player, light a candle or two, and we'd kick back for a nice evening. It was okay to fall apart at Anna's. She was a survivor too, and as I was falling apart, she'd let me. She had that deep-seeing eye. *It's okay, it's okay, you're making sense, breathe with me, okay.* She was slow and kind and funny. A loner, the way I was. Happy in her apartment by herself, cooking food on the stove, getting greasy working on a bike in its stand, taping some songs onto a cassette from another for a friend, going for long bike rides or walks by herself. We made plans; we were going to start a business on wheels, a combination bike repair and coffee/smoothie stand. You could call a cell phone and get her, and we'd bike to where your bike had broken down, and she'd work on it while I fixed you a drink and rubbed your back. I tried to call her again.

Then, I remembered. I had that phone number Alys had given me, in my book, the number for central intake into the shelter system. I called it.

"Name?" I gave it, even though I thought, *What if I don't want to?*

"Can I go to Nellie's?" I asked. That was the nice shelter, the one in an old Victorian house in the east end that had rooms with just a couple of beds, not a fucked-up place with mats on the floor.

"No, they're full. Why do you need to go to a shelter?"

I told her my partner had hit me and she made me go over it again a couple of times. "What? He did what exactly? What's your social insurance number?" That's when I lost it.

"I don't have one," I told the voice on the other end of the phone.

"Well, then we can't process you into the system."

That was it. I hung up. How long would it take for Rafael to come after me? How long would it take for him to catch the bus? Was he killing himself right now, as we spoke? I had my little notebook of names and phone numbers. I called them until I got somebody. Marcus. "Hang on, I'll come right now. Can you meet me someplace? The Coffee Time in the market. Fine, I'll see you there."

I waited in that Coffee Time for four hours. I took a cab there, which was decadent, but I was scared shitless and figured that would shake Rafael for sure. Went to the john and tried to clean up with paper towels. Sat in a booth with a double-double and a toasted coconut doughnut reading the same book over and over, *Born Palestinian, Born Black*, that Rafael had given me for Christmas. It was thin, but I needed something to read to keep the folks in the doughnut shop at bay. Trying for nonchalant: *Of course it is perfectly normal for me to be here, staying up all night in a Coffee Time. I am being a bohemian who keeps strange late-night hours. I do not have a ripped-up knee, a freaked-out expression on my face, an attempt to keep it together, to keep my cheeks from moving into sobs, to keep my face quiet and blank and don't-fuck-with-me.* Marcus showed up with Siue Yin at three a.m., just when I was thinking about giving up and had pumped a few quarters into the payphone looking for him with no luck. I was going over my options: walk to a nearby park and sleep under a tree? Try Anna again? A motel was out of the question; I had the twenty bucks on me when I left the apartment, and that was rapidly depleted from the cab ride and coffee and phone calls. Marcus and Siue Yin seemed altogether too goddamn happy when they walked in.

"Sorry it took a while, we walked!" Marcus chirped. I glared at him. This was not a time for conserving fossil fuels, was what I thought.

"Let's get out of here and go to the park. Siue Yin got her herbal first-aid kit. Maybe she can check you out. Are you hurt anywhere?"

"Uh, no. Not really. My knee and my back. My back feels pretty wrenched. But no." And that seemed to make it worse. I felt like a liar. I didn't have any physical scars, just a scraped knee, and what was that? To make such a big deal out of it, drag these guys from their houses. They were looking at me with wide eyes, real caring. And delicate. Like I was delicate, needed to be talked to gently because I could start bawling or losing it at any moment.

But we did it, we got out of there and walked to the park and sat on benches under floodlights next to punk kids curled up with their dogs sleeping in the drained wading pool. Siue Yin carefully washed out the grit and cinders from my knee, sponged it with something cool, and taped it up.

And then I started to cry. I'd tranced out a bit when she was washing my knee. Couldn't really feel Marcus put his arm around me. I knew Rafael was killing himself, right then as we spoke. I sobbed and sobbed and could feel something let go. Him. His spirit. Finally. Dying like he always said he wanted to, like he always said he would. I held my knees, rocked back and forth, saw black and purple from behind my eyes, squinched shut. I could feel it, feel his soul where it had my solar plexus in its fist; I felt it unclench and whirl away.

I went to Siue Yin's place. We walked there. With a giggle, she asked, "Are you up for it?" She was letting me stay there, but I barely knew her and was a bit wary. She and Rajiv had been the ones who lectured me about my bisexual privilege, about how I shouldn't hug or mack on Rafael. And now, here I was, an obvious example of where doing boys will get you, beaten up in a paisley skirt at five a.m. The sun was coming up as we walked to her house on Concord—a nice street, probably the nicest in the west end, with its dripping trees and feeling of peace. But her apartment was a basement, all dank carpet.

"Sit down, sit down, sleep anywhere you want," Siue Yin said, in her Hong Kong accent. I put the bag I'd had with me down on the sofa, the stupid hot-pink and lime-green, fake-looking Guatemalan bag with two straps and an open top that, right then, carried all my worldly goods. "Go to sleep for a while, if you want to."

I did, sort of, lying on the sofa in all my clothes under the covers. I twisted and turned and finally gave in, uneasy.

I woke up late and called Marcus, who'd told me to call him any time. He was being supportive. We got falafel down the block and ran into Ernesto, who chewed his falafel solemnly as he listened to what had gone down.

"Do you want me to have a healing circle with him?" he asked. Sure. I didn't really know what that meant, but it sounded good. He nodded seriously, chewing. Ernesto was older, in his forties already, though it was easy to forget, as he didn't look any older than anyone else or broadcast Creepy Older Man. He fit in with the whole posse of Latino radicals in their twenties and thirties who hung with Rafael and me. But he was more serious and grown up, you could tell; worked at the CBC doing serious journalism. He nodded and looked out the window, his eyes already somewhere else.

But it was Desh Pardesh that weekend, which made things sort of extra complicated. Desh was this radical South Asian arts and politics festival. Very queer, very working-class, with every kind of South Asian, performances in the housing projects and the queer theater. I was supposed to cover the whole thing for the local college radio station. They'd given me my own handheld cassette recorder for this. I made my way down to Buddies, where it was being held, for the first night. In the same outfit. I was cringing with embarrassment. *They're going to think I'm some white girl who's wearing a paisley skirt to be authentic or supportive or something*, and indeed this is what some of them thought, I found out years later. I was too shy to ask about putting a line into the mic, so I just squatted in front of the stage, holding the recorder up as far as it could go for a couple of hours.

Desh was a catastrophe of brownness. All the shades of South Asian browns. All the kinds of eyebrows there were. Sexy queer femme aunties in their forties, wearing dark blood-red saris and arms full of silver bangles, smoking cigars outside, and staring at you. Amina in her creamy white tailored suit, her tits and ass poured into it, hair curled perfectly, radiant in her fatness. Anjali with her shaved head growing in patchily, green dye starting to wash out the way green Manic Panic does, so the hair looks like it's moldy, rocking the femmest shalwar from the last wedding she had to go to. Vashti had a butch boi rooster cut and wore a lungi. All the accents rolled out, relaxed. I stared at all of it, trying to hide my desperate desire to fit into it, to be accepted. I stared at it hungrily, eating it up with my eyes, looking for parts I could make mine. Things I could be. Things that would work on my body.

Every place outside of Desh, I was brown, immigrant, something. But here, I was white. I was some dumb white girl, some dumb half-and-half girl. There was brown and there was white. And there were five million Punjabi girls who maybe had been working-class once but weren't now, or maybe had always had money, perfect threaded eyebrows, and a lot of bitchy fake-polite attitude. "So, what interested you in this festival?" "Oh, so you're just a mutt!" "I mean, with your features, I wondered why you were here... but now I see!" Tinkling laughter. I ate the free good food; trays of sabzi, saag paneer, and tubs full of samosas.

I still went to every panel at Desh Pardesh. In one room at the queer center, there were mats spread out all over the floor and this girl, Sheila. She was half too, and she was a yoga teacher. She talked about her thesis, about yoga as a form of decolonial healing, about how capitalism was making money off it. Sheila had been told she had the perfect Bengali hip structure for poses in yoga school, but when she questioned the racism or brought up feeling uncomfy that three white girls in a week had changed their names to Sita, Rita, and Amrita, her teacher told her she wasn't really South Asian, so what did she know? She talked about women of color in her people-of-color yoga classes who said they wouldn't do yoga ordinarily because they were afraid to close their eyes in a room full of white people when the teacher told them to close their eyes and relax. I knew that fear. She had us lay on the mats and breathe and do basic postures, slowly. I felt myself coming back in. There was something in my hips that wanted to cry all the time that felt soothed.

On the third night, as we were ready to get going, Siue Yin said, "Uh, Leah, I need to ask you something." She'd found some girl who wanted to go home with her and was wondering, with lots of fits and starts, if I could find someplace else to stay that night. What could I say? *Sure, I'll figure something out.* I turned my back on all the radical South Asians and started to walk. I tried Anna again.

"Superdiva, what's wrong?" Anna asked. She said she'd meet me. I was in a phone booth outside OISE talking to her, and all of a sudden I saw Rafael on his bike. He skidded to a stop and stared at me. I stared at him. I was trapped in the booth. He made something, some kind of pleading gesture. I shook my head, *no, no*, moved my arm, *go away*. He nodded and peddled off. His eyes were tortured.

"Leah? What's going on?"

"Rafael, he was just here on his bike, he stopped, I said he should go away. Can you meet me somewhere in between?"

It was a long walk to where we agreed to meet. I was really tired and was still carrying everything in the world on my back and feeling like I looked like a hippie. I still had a scraped knee with the bandage on it and one outfit. It would have been a great time for social services to swoop by in a van and offer me soup right then, but as usual, social services had bad timing.

Also, it was Saturday night in June, and there were tons of yahoos out on the street, especially near the university. My hips hurt. I was putting one foot in front of the other. I think I finally broke down and took a cab part of the way there when it became clear that walking fast and shaving the usual hour-and-a-half-long walk to forty-five minutes was not an option. A cab felt incredibly bougie, but I was also spooked, eyes all over my skin—what if I ran into Rafael on his bike again?

When I came into the park, I saw Anna sitting on a picnic table, drumming her fingers on the wood. Her eyes held me steady as I walked towards her. We said the usual heys, and then I asked her how I looked. I honestly had no idea.

"I thought to myself when I saw you," Anna said, "that's a woman who's walking out of hell. And she's already seen it and she's walking anyway."

We went back to her house, and she fixed me hot cocoa in a pan, half milk, half water, so you stretch it. Cocoa and cinnamon.

I tried to talk about it. The story was right on the tip on my tongue, told perfectly in my brain, but I couldn't quite get the words out. *I got out, he's fucked up, but that's no excuse.* I didn't say, *I thought he died. I thought he killed himself like he always said he would.* But I felt like he really did die that night. Somehow.

Anna and I slept on her double bed until the light started slanting in the window.

My mom always said, "If you're a smart woman, you'll see it coming and get out. Only stupid women don't see that."

In the morning, Rafael called Anna's. He'd also called last

night, right after I got off the phone, she told me. He'd said, "I just saw Leah in the phone booth. She shook her head. What does that mean?"

"It means she wants you to leave her alone."

He called again, and she asked if I wanted to talk to him, and I thought, *what the hell.* I was in control for this second. I had something he wanted. Me.

Anna needed her space, so I moved again, to Jim's. He was the aging anarchist head of *Prison News Service*, the newspaper I wrote for. I'd been at his co-op in the east end; it was a pretty, low brick two-storey with gardens in the back, wood floors, and enough room for five people to eat at the dining room table. The production company for the paper was in the basement along with all the years of *Prison News Service* back issues in boxes on the floor. I slept on the couch. It was a doable walk after crouching at the front of Buddies taping Desh again. Later the tapes would turn out to be unusable; I'd moved too much and there was too much static.

Jim talked a lot about the politics of abuse; he was a survivor too, so I thought his couch would be a good bet, and it was for a while. Jim had come back from an anarchist farm in 1972 that was populated by all trustafarians except for him. He'd screamed fuck it and gotten a good union job as a meter reader. He walked around all day, was done by three, and had a good amount of time in the evenings to run a paper. That was one strategy. Maybe I could become a meter reader.

When Rafael and I finally talked, we met near Desh at a weird little artificial grotto on the Ryerson campus. It was partially shaded by a cement bridge, and there were hordes of businessy first-generation students walking around, even though it was June.

"Hi."

"Hi."

"It's good to see you."

"You, too." It was. My body wanted to touch his. Malcolm X T-shirt, stubble, doo rag, smile.

I stared at my feet for a while. Then I looked up and these words came out: "I want the house back. You were the one who hit me. I don't think *I* should have to try and find a place to live."

"I can't believe you said that. Do you know how much it hurts me to hear you talk about ... *that?*"

"That?! I'm not supposed to talk about *that!* You mean you *hitting* me? Oh, poor you! I'm the one who still has a fucked-up knee and back! I don't give a fuck what you feel bad about!"

He looked away and down, toward the weird little grotto. Said quietly, "You're right. I'm sorry."

We stared off into space some more. I checked out a little, felt my body just click off.

Abruptly, he said, "I'll still marry you, you know. I feel like I have a duty, a responsibility, to help you get across the border."

I looked up. "Okay, but we're never going to be lovers again. You know that. Right?"

"Yeah. I know." Pause. Brown blue eyeball stare, on the steps of the Ryerson waterfall.

"Okay. As long as you understand that." I looked him in the eye. Maybe if I stared hard enough, said it the right way, what I wanted to be true would happen.

"I'll talk to Ernesto," he said. "I can probably move into Homeboy house."

"You want to live with those fools?"

"You want me to live with white people?"

"Fine." I didn't really care, as long as I got the house in the divorce.

And then we talked. The same long conversation. Abuse and racism and internalized racism and colonialism and colorism and self-hatred and the violence our folks had survived, how it all came together into one huge force that combined the psychiatric industrial complex, the prison industrial complex, the theft of First Nations land, and how we ourselves were also colonized; we were immigrants, not settlers.

He rose up when the sun was going down. "Can I walk you to the streetcar?"

"Sure." When we got to the Dundas streetcar and it stopped next to all the construction where they had torn down the Island Jerk place where you could get a $1.99 lunch special, I said, "It's okay. Just get on the streetcar with me."

When I moved out of Jim's after the week was up—when I passed the key to Jim and took the bus home—I walked up to it quietly, looking all around. I put my key in the lock, then the other lock, and went up the stairs warily. Going through all the rooms, checking everything out, I let out a deep breath. I was alone, and the door was locked, and only I had the key.

15. The Amethyst Room

There's a room like an altar in the middle of the broken-down house. Amethyst, like the color of the womb I would've grown inside if I had a colored mother. That's how I think of it. There's a lumpy plum-colored double futon I picked off the street with the duvet I hauled with me on the floor. A big wardrobe, groaning open, was left there that makes me feel rich; no furniture, milk crates, things that were taken from junk.

This is where I dream for hours. The train hoots by. A window in the bathroom opens onto the wild backyard jungle of burdock, wild grape, dandelion, narrow bands of dirt that grow peas lettuce and greens, motherwort, tomatillos, tomatoes, and a wild shaggy weed tree. There are at least twenty feral cats living by the tracks. I dream for hours. It takes me four hours to get off the futon to go to the bathroom and have hot baths with sea salt to pull everything toxic out of my body.

This is my first home. The first place I can shut the door and when I do, everything exhales.

I tried to find this place for years in New York. Even before *Sex in the City* ultra-gentrification, I could never afford anything. They wouldn't rent to me as a student on financial aid with parents who were helping out and a Barnes & Noble job. But I pictured a railroad flat, with three little rooms glowing yellow, and a door that shut.

This place is a womb where I regrew myself. A starfish. Someone in neonatal.

The night before I put the twenty-two-page manila envelope in the mail to my mother I had this dream:

I was floating in the sky. Way up in the inky black. I could feel all the ancestors around me, hovering.

I asked them, "Is what I think about my parents, about everything, true?"

I didn't hear, but felt, the word YES slamming into my body. Echoing from everywhere around me.

And then I was falling, so many millions of miles an hour back down.

I woke with a thump as I fell back down on the bed.

There were stabbing pains in my cunt. There were times when I felt that my three-year-old self was walking next to me. That girl—her short legs, soft bowl-cut, huge hazel eyes that are all the way present and disassociated—I walk the alleyways with her. I hold her hand.

16. Paula: Toronto, 1997

When Paula, Rafael's mother, came to visit, she brought us things. She brought us a blender, a tent, an Indian print bedspread to cover the one big-ass window in our fucked-up, one-room, put down-the-café-con-leche-and-there-are-ten-roaches-in-it-five-minutes-later apartment. She fed us a lot and always paid.

When Paula was eighteen, she'd already known how to field strip an M16, back when she was pregnant with Rafael in the first year of the revolution in Chile. But after the coup, jail, the refugee camp in Czechoslovakia where Rafael was born, and twenty years of her husband, she was a tight quiet woman who worked seventy-five-hour weeks at a massage therapy clinic and meditated the rest of the time. I knew we reminded her of herself when she first came to Canada, fighting over whether it was right to sell the bus ticket we found on the curb to somebody for $1.85.

When Paula called me this time, I didn't think twice about saying yes. We went to Kensington Market and walked among junkies, hippies, and brown people, in the smoggy dust. She bought me pupusas from the Guatemalteco stand and fair trade coffee from the hippie café. Then we walked over to the park where the punks slept on picnic tables under curved pine trees and there was a kids' wading pool mostly free of piss.

I stared off at the swing-set, remembering six months ago, when Rafael slammed my ass into his hands each time he pumped me on the swing. I was wearing my tight black satin slip and boots, and I admired the curve of my cocoa-butter-brown thighs as I swung into the full moon. But on this day, I looked like hell. I was rocking a dumpy blue-and-white print, knee-length hippie sundress that Paula had brought me last time and a thin fringe of hair still fucked-up from where Mom had cut it all off six months earlier.

Paula kicked off her sandals, nodded for me to do the same, and walked me to the water, linking her arm through mine. We walked in small steps around the edge of the pool. Kids screaming through the water zoomed past us, throwing shit.

Halfway around the pool, she turned and stared into my eyes, cupped her palms around my face. She was so poetic and dramatic, like her eyeliner, a Chilean Stevie Nicks. "So, tell me. Why aren't you two together, anymore?"

"Well," I said. I paused, then blurted out, "He was violent. More than once. He hit me."

She dropped her hands, dropped her smile. Her expression was angrier than any I'd seen on her face. She started to walk again, faster, without looking at me anymore.

"He hit you how many times? For how long?"

"Uh. For the past three months."

She snorted. "Three months? Three months is nothing. You

think that's bad? I've been dealing with it for twenty years."

I turned to stare at the side of her head. She still wouldn't look at me. "I'm sorry, Paula." I didn't know what I was apologizing for. Her for taking it for twenty years. Me for leaving.

"Yes, well." She breathed in, exhaled in a whoosh. "Why are you staying here? Couldn't you go back to your parents? Doesn't your mother have cancer?"

"We're not talking right now. There's a lot of abuse in my family." I said it pretty fast—theresalotofabuseinmyfamily.

"What do you mean? Like this, hitting?"

"No, sexual abuse."

She drew in a breath. Then looked sympathetic, and like, *Oh, it all makes sense now.* Why I was so fucked-up about her son hitting me just a couple of times. "Your father?"

"No. No, my mother." Why the fuck did I say that.

"Your *mother*?" She turned and stared at me again, horrified. The sympathy was gone. She just looked at me like I was crazy and like that explained everything even more. Her son had chosen a really confused, fucked-up girl who already had violence smeared on her body like shit. Like shit you saw on *Oprah.*

"Yeah, my mother." I tried to keep walking, but she grabbed my hand so hard I couldn't move.

"But that's unheard of."

Yeah, well, it's heard of by me. "Yeah, well."

"How?"

That was one thing I learned from talking to the ladies on the crisis line. "I don't really feel comfortable talking about the details."

"Oh." She exhaled. "I still don't see why you don't go back to the States. Everyone wants to go there, and you can."

I knew I couldn't explain it to her, how it'd just been six months, but I felt like the US didn't even exist for me anymore. Where would I stay? Luna's place? Vandana's? I hadn't talked to her since last summer, so could I beg her to save me from one more jam? This wasn't a lot, but at least here when shit had gone down, there had been couches.

The parks people rolled up in their little cart. One of them waded into the water and reached down to pull the plug. The water started to drain back from the edge in little ripples. Paula said that she had to get going soon, had to go to Homeboy House to meet her son, my ex, the one who was doing the hitting.

Before she left, she kissed me on the cheek and looked into my eyes. "I have one piece of advice for you, *carita*. Don't let go that easy. He won't always be like this."

After Paula walked away, I sat on the bench near the swing. Fingered my fucked-up hair. Thought of the photo Rafael had shown me, the only one left from his childhood. In the picture, Paula had long Joan Bacz wings of dark hair and thick, black eyeliner. Her fingers held a cigarette, and she stared at the camera with a bright, cracked, *everything's fine!* smile. Alejandro, Rafael's father, squatted at the table like a frog, with his heavyset face and loopy curls, holding his cigarette between two fingers. You could feel how close he was to about-to-explode. I could anyway; I recognized the look. Rafael sat below them. He was maybe seven or eight, with a haze of brown curls in a big poofy 'fro around his face. His eyes were frozen, staring away, out of the picture to somewhere else, maybe into the fifth dimension.

After Paula left, I spent that summer working at a landscaping job that Anna had gotten me. I tried to grow vegetables in the backyard that my downstairs neighbor, the conspiracy theorist, swore wouldn't grow because the CIA had put radiation in the house. Walked to the library and back. Cooked meals from the store I discovered at Bloor and Ossington that had "pesticide-free" veggies and fruits from a farm that didn't spray but wasn't certified. Peaches from the Niagara escarpment, bunches of spinach, baskets of snap beans, concord grapes, melon. Then cheap pasta and rice and dairy from the bulk store next door. A blueberry muffin and a coffee for a once-a-week treat. Anna and I took a free feminist lady self-defense course at a Jewish community center down the block from the landscaping job. I impressed all the ladies with my tales of breaking the grip of an abuser. I didn't tell them I was still talking to him.

The wedding was in September. It took a while for me to get the money together; a hundred dollars for the license and another fifty to pay off the radical Catholic priest, a friend of Jim's who'd agreed to do the ceremony. Although he wasn't too happy about it; he'd been pleasant at first, when we went to meet him in his nice house in Riverdale around the corner from Jim's co-op, but when he boomed out, "So what are two anarchists doing getting married?" and we'd said, "For immigration," his smile had disappeared. It hadn't occurred to me that some people saw marriage as something serious, not just a piece of paper that you got at the border. He finally said he'd do it if we wrote the vows and did all the work and he just had to read them. So I did. I wrote our vows on the Mac Classic. There was a lot of John Trudell and Buffy Sainte-Marie.

On my wedding day, I wore the French Connection dress I'd bought on sale because it made me feel like a real New Yorker, to have a little black dress. It hung a little loose but was still more appropriate than my jeans and fourteen-hole Docs or anything else I owned. Anjali and Tidy looked more dressed-up than we did, Anjali in her Pakistani wedding kameez, Tidy in his '60s Black Militant uniform, vest, and kufi. I had planned this perfectly. I knew we needed photos, and it had to look legit, so I was a little worried when Rafael showed up in his murder-ones, green prison dress shirt, and black jeans. But there was a little painted wooden arch by a native plants display, painted with a picture of a stream and words describing the creek that used to flow here. I figured that if we took the wedding photos in front of the arch, it would look like we had built this specially constructed thing for the ceremony. Maybe it would make up for the fact that the bride was wearing black and the groom looked like a thug.

The people arrived. Rafael's uncle Ernesto, with the white wife and kids, then Jim, showed up dragging a bag of Portuguese roasted chicken. White-dread Phillip brought a bunch of lychees and grapes. It looked like everyone was taking this more seriously than I was. I started to freak out.

I looked at Rafael. "C'mere for a sec," I said to him and took him by the hand. At first we were walking, but then I started to run, dragging him with me, leaving behind all the wedding guests, the fruit, chicken, and little archway. We stopped by some trees, chests heaving. He looked at me, eyebrows quirked.

"Promise me you'll never call me your wife," I said. "That's all I want to know."

He grinned back at me. "I promise, pepita."

17. The Winter You Are So Broke

That winter I was broke. The fold of Canadian dollar bills from under-the-table labor in the empty yogurt container in the fridge got thinner every day. I tried to survive without taking anything out of it, but I needed groceries, I needed to get the fuck out of the house and walk down to the Price Chopper's orange and blue beacon at the broke people's mall at Dupont and Dufferin.

Being broke means you can buy lotion but not conditioner, conditioner but not lotion, you can use one for both. You can use cheap olive oil for everything. It means you know how much everything costs. Falafel is $1.99 at Ghazele or the spot with the good fries down at Church and Wellesley, in between the queer strip and St Jamestown, and more importantly, between Jim's co-op and my apartment miles away in the west end. Even though public transit was only two dollars, and sometimes we had it, it meant waiting, shaking with cold on the street corner for an hour. The cops had just started taking Plexiglas out of the bus shelters so no one could sleep there, and the wind would come screaming down the street from off the river and kill us. One time, to keep warm, Rafael and I started to jump up and down and scream "WE ALL LIVE IN A FASCIST POLICE STATE" to the tune of "Yellow Submarine".

We tried to convince ourselves that one leather jacket plus one quilted vest lined with fake synthetic sheepskin bought at one of those stores in the Market that catered to construction workers, plus a million hoodies, would somehow make up for the fact that we didn't have any down winter coats.

This moment of truth came one day after the winter, when Angel and Keisha and Rafael came over to my house. I was wearing a tank top and a zip-up sweatshirt despite the cold. I'd bought flour and yeast at Strictly Bulk for seventy-five cents and made homemade pita bread out of the *Laurel's Kitchen Bread Book*. When Keisha arrived, her glance fell on my upper arms. I looked down.

"Wow, I'm thin," I said, surprised. I had always been thin, always had a fast metabolism that burned off whatever I ate and made me speedy. I thought that I was hanging in there all through that hard winter, bundling up and walking to the Price Chopper or the Strictly Bulk, waiting for spring. I thought I had it down. But as Keisha and I both looked at the bare brown sticks of my upper arms, we thought differently. "Yeah, you're thin alright," she said. "It's kind of ... disturbing."

Rafael told me about the weekly jobs working in the Foodshare warehouse. Foodshare was a community-based organization that prepared Good Food Boxes, which were big forest-green Rubbermaid containers filled with nutritious, seasonal fruits and veggies that could be bought for fifteen dollars. If you went to Foodshare's Eastern Avenue warehouse and packed boxes all day, they didn't pay you, but they did feed you really good vegetarian food, including some kind of warm dessert, and you got to go home with a full box of food. They also offered an organic box, which was thirty dollars, and an Afri-Can Food basket, which had culturally specific foods and a lot of ital produce, like yams, plantains, and greens, and tons of cheap but delicious juice oranges. Rafael packed for them sometimes, and later, in January, he gave his free box to me. At first, I protested, but he just looked at me and shook his head. "You take it. You need it more than me," he said. I ate from that box for a month. When I had bus tokens—and I got really angry that they didn't always provide tokens—I made it to the warehouse to pack. It was full of humming conveyor belts and vegetables and lots of people on welfare or disability, or who didn't qualify for either but couldn't find a job. We were all working eight-hour shifts for the promise of some broccoli. I did it, but I also wondered whether this kind of Oliver Twist workhouse scenario was going to be my future.

When you're that broke, your perspective changes. One hundred and eight-five pennies seems like a huge amount of money—the weight of that copper. Rent was $525, the most enormous sum of money I had to sweat and sweat and sweat to scrape up each month, and then it all went to the landlord, just so I could have 400 square feet to breathe in, and a door to close.

Rafael and I came up with a lot of hare-brained schemes to make money. We lined up at a City of Toronto warehouse at five in the morning to register for the occasional snow-shoveling pool. I didn't have a social insurance number yet, but I wrote "in progress" on my application. Rafael swore we could make twenty-two dollars an hour working there, and it seemed like an unfathomably huge sum of money.

That winter, we spent a lot of time at Rafael's cozy little bachelor apartment in the basement of a big old house on Springhurst. It was a single ten-by-ten-foot room with a two-burner stove and a mini fridge. There was room for a desk, a bookcase made out of thick wooden planks and bricks that Rafael's dad brought home from the lumberyard at Ossington, and the same damn futon mattress. We spent a lot of time there making tea or coffee, eating oranges, reading poems out loud from *Aloud: Voices of the Nuyorican Poet's Cafe*, and listening to records on the turntable or tapes that we loaded up into the boom box.

It was a cold-ass winter. The wait for the Dufferin bus home at three a.m. just about killed me. Sometimes I slept over. It was warm, and there were oranges.

18. The Letter

Winter of 1998. I wrote the longest letter ever, one of those incest-survivor letters where you try to tell everything—everything. Where you think that if you write it just the right way, your family is going to get it, and everything's going be okay.

I photocopied Chrystos and Sapphire poems into the letter. I probably looked like a giant, twenty-two-year-old, desperate, asshole, child-woman who insisted on praying, *She has cancer. Maybe we can all finally cut the shit and be real if she's going to die. If the stakes are that high.*

My mother's cancer had come back, and the call had come in late fall. Both of my parents were on the phone. "Just come home, Leah." My mom's voice, crying, and my dad's voice, stern but breaking. "Come home. And take care of her."

I could see that future stretching in front of me. Me home, the weird older daughter, back in my room. Hanging out with my mother. Taking care of my mother. Bargaining for an evening out now and then. Still no driver's license. Never leaving.

It would be like when I was sixteen, insisting that I was an adult, except that I wasn't, in some ways. Was I an adult? Or was I something else? Would I ever grow up?

Instead, I wrote that letter. I sweated it. Worked on it like it was work.

One winter day, I put it in a manila envelope and addressed it to Worcester, MA, 01602, and walked to a mailbox. Rafael and Keisha were with me. I stopped, paused, opened the slot, and then slid it in. Closed it. Could hear it land on the pile of mail inside. The door closing on the old and opening on a brand-new life.

No turning back.

Breaking into a mailbox is a felony.

Little white snowflakes landed on my shoulders. Doing a little dance all around us.

Part Three

HOW TO COME BACK

Later, during the question and answer session, a worried
West African immigrant brother asked her, "But after colonization, what do we do? What if our parents and grandparents
refuse to tell us anything? They don't want to talk about the old
days. They are afraid. Or they don't remember."

She looked at him with great compassion and said, "Then
you go back further, to the source," and her hands swept back
with assurance to the beginning of time, the birth of life.

The brother nodded, still confused, but comforted, and
I was dazzled by the recognition that nothing is truly lost,
just hidden. We are the sum of all our ancestors. Some speak
louder than others, but they all remain present, alive in our
very blood and bone.

—*Lisa Kahaleole Hall,* "Eating Salt" in NAMES WE CALL HOME:
AUTOBIOGRAPHY ON RACIAL IDENTITY

19. Healing Justice Mix Tape

Bikini Kill: "DemiRep"

African Head Charge: "Heading to Glory"

Fun-da-mental: "Sistah India" and "Wrath of the Black Man"

John Trudell: anything from *Blue Indians* or *Johnny Damas and Me*

Asian Dub Foundation: "Naxalite"

Joy Harjo: "For Anna Mae Pictou Aquash"

Buffy Sainte-Marie: "I'm Going Home"

Method Man and Mary J. Blige: "You're All I Need"

Tribe Called Quest: "Stressed Out"

Me'shell Ndegeocello: "Ecclesiastes: Free My Heart"

20. Hard Times Survival Dinner No. 1, Toronto, 1998

Ingredients:
  black-eyed peas or dhal or black beans
  brown rice
  sweet potatoes
  greens
  Optional: 1 chicken leg
  Optional: interchangeable cake

There's a bean, a grain, an orange and green vegetable, and something sweet. Flava, always.

Instructions: Either wait til you get paid $130 from your under-the-table job on Friday or take twenty dollars from the roll of money hidden in the empty yogurt container in the fridge. Pause a long time before you take that money from the fridge. You can only spend twenty dollars each week on food. Less is better.

If it's freezing, and your body is too fucked-up to walk to Bloor and Ossington, walk to the Price Chopper, where you can score the cheapest beans in the Ethnic Foods aisle with all the Cedars and Mr. Gouda's cans. The veggies are pretty cheap too, but the quality is substandard. Trade-off: often there is enough left to purchase some bulla cakes for two dollars, as a treat, and it is within walking distance, saving you the bus fare. Or go through the change jar. If you know you're short, just get together a shitload of pennies. If you dump them all in the bus's change receptacle, they won't check, just wave you through, especially if you work to look as not-poor as possible. Walk on the bus like a queen, then smile nicely.

If the weather is nice or you don't have the $3.70 for the bus, or if you're really holding out for quality vegetables, drag the granny cart to Bloor and Ossington. Make it to that greengrocer, the one that has rows of vegetables with hand-lettered cardboard signs reading, "Pesticide Free," from a farm in Niagara that doesn't spray but can't afford certification. Once you're at the store, remember that you don't have to pay more than a dollar for collards! Collards are best—you can make the most things with them—but chard or kale is okay.

The bulk store carries thirty-nine cent a pound pancake mix. One Organic Valley quart of two percent milk is $2.39. Oatmeal is so cheap, and the Susun Weed herb book says it'll help you stay calm and resilient. Flour to make bread with is thirty cents a pound. (Making bread takes time, but you have a lot of it, and it's much, much cheaper than buying it. Get three pounds of flour.) Rice. Dried black beans take fucking forever to cook but are 300 percent cheaper than canned. Get a can of coconut milk, or better, one of those Grace brand bars of dried coconut cream in a solid block; it doesn't go bad.

Afterward, maybe splurge and spend a dollar on a coffee at the bulk store and, for a big splurge, another dollar on a blueberry muffin. Rest for a minute. Put the bags down. After a while, put them in the cart. Walk home. You can do it. You forgot coffee! The cheapest is $4.99 a pound in the Market. Eggs are $1.99 for six; they're your treat. Peppermint tea, Three Leaves brand, is $1.99 for twenty bags. Scrawl all of this down on a used envelope when you're making your list. If you're seventeen cents over, sometimes the guy will let you take it anyway. Be young. Be cute. Down on your luck. Not permanent.

Every item has to have multiple purposes. Look up calorie counts in the back of the *New Laurel's Kitchen* cookbook, where there are charts of calories and fat and vitamins designed for hippies trying to be mad low fat. You have a different goal. Try to get up to 1,500 a day.

Make it home, with stops. Make it up the stairs. Sink into the old sage-green armchair you found on the street. It puffs out dust. Rest.

Soak black-eyeds overnight, or cheat and boil them and let them sit with a plate on top of the pot for an hour. Throw the stinky soaking water away. Cook the beans with a bay leaf, allspice, sea salt. Make rice. Stab knife into yam and stick in oven. Enjoy how warm the kitchen is because of this. Chop greens and garlic. Cook up with some hot sauce, soy sauce, vinegar, and pepper. Mix cooked peas into brown rice, mix in chopped, dried coconut and slivered green onions.

Fill a huge stoneware plate from your parents' 1970s set that they don't use anymore, that you got into the van when you went back to get your shit, with all of the above. Maybe have one chicken leg from the ninety-nine cent Mennonite butcher. Also on the maybe list: homemade oatmeal cookies (bulk store margarine, oatmeal, brown sugar, flour) or interchangeable cake (half a cup brown sugar, half a cup margarine, one cup flour, baking powder, and a cup of apples, pears, mashed sweet potatoes, or squash—whatever you have—and spices.)

Take it to the green armchair. Look out the window. Give thanks for this, for a plate filled with an orange vegetable and a dark green one; color, protein, and flavor. You cooked this on two dollars. Fill yourself. Let yourself rest.

21. Chronic Fatigue Immune Deficiency Syndrome

I took three years off sex. Three years that were supposed to be my prime time, by somebody's rulebook. Between 1997, when I broke up with Rafael, to 2000, I was in the wet and the raw. Sex was the last thing on my mind, for the first time in my life.

I shoved all my growing-back hair in a hoodie and went for long walks. I dug up burdock and dandelion and put them in the cheapest vodka I could find at the liquor store and made tincture out of them. Walking the alleyways and railroad tracks became a game to me, seeing how long I could go without talking to people. I was happiest when I didn't have a body. I had been all body, all gender for a while. I needed some time off from having a body in order to figure out what kind of relationship I would have with one when I got back to it.

I was also doing this because I was sick as hell, which, with classic chronically ill/disabled double consciousness, I wasn't letting myself see. I was sleeping between twelve and seventeen hours a day. Sometimes it took me an hour to gather the strength together to get off the bed, go down the hallway, and get to the toilet.

It's hard to describe the gray gray purply gray of chronic

fatigue to anyone who hasn't been there. Just imagine: the oxygen you breathe every day? Imagine that all of a sudden it's filled with carbon dioxide instead. Or maybe that it's just sixty percent of the oxygen content you're used to breathing. Maybe forty percent. Like you're on a leaky spaceship. Like you're in the Himalayas and you still have so far to climb.

Imagine that your brain is spacey, and thinking itself takes many times as long as you are used to.

Imagine that you are moving through what feels like wet cement, thinking through wet cement. Imagine that eating, cooking, and shitting all take valuable energy, of which you have a very small bank account.

Also, there was a lot of fucking pain and ache throughout my body, which corresponded to absolutely nothing organic and related, and there was not a lot I could do about it.

Imagine you don't have money, so you have to walk every-where, so your labor is walking. You bank your energy so that, once a week, you can drag your granny cart from Dupont and Bartlett to the Strictly Bulk, load up on staples, rest for a while, then drag the cart back home. You plan your meals for the week. Some weeks it is ten dollars, and you have to get really creative.

Sometimes your legs give out, and you can't walk anymore. Your balance is fucked; you want to throw up when you're creeping up and down the stairs. You have to rest after you walk a block. You don't have the words to explain this to anyone. Are you just tired? Haven't you always been tired? Are you just lazy?

You can't go to the doctor. Your friend tells you that you'll be denied supplemental insurance if there's anything on your record. Your other friend and the legal clinic tell you that Immigration won't let disabled people into the country; they think we're an unnatural drain on that lovely Canadian free health care social service system. And you're trying to stay under the radar of every single government system, period. That's why you don't hit the food bank that often or the drop-ins or any of the social programs designed to help you. You have to be low-profile so immigration has other people to punish, so you just look like some girl from America with a BA and English proficiency and a white last name married to a boy with some priors and a CSIS file but probably not about to be a burden on the Canadian social welfare state, which she couldn't be anyway, as all immigrants who come here sign a form that says we're not allowed to access any state money whatsoever.

So you don't. But you go back and forth in your head. Are you lazy? Are you crazy? Is there something really wrong with you?

Sometimes I would look at my copy of *Our Bodies, Ourselves: For the New Century* in the Some Common and Uncommon Medical Problems section. There was a subsection on Fibromyalgia and Chronic Fatigue, and I'd wonder if I had that. Because it kind of fucking sounded like I had it.

But wasn't it just a made up disease?

Made up just like abuse memory.

People with fibromyalgia and/or CF/IDS have a high tendency to also have abuse memories. True fact.

Disability doesn't know its name at first, when it's acquired later in life. It's still you in here, but you feel different. The words surface slowly in the fatigued brain.

I was supposed to be famous at twenty-three and fucking and fixed, but I wasn't. I was doing this instead. Lying down. Being sick. Remembering. Being crazy.

How did I get better?

I didn't fake it. I couldn't fake it. I couldn't fake that everything was okay and I wasn't crazy and sick. I couldn't hold down a job. I couldn't drink or smoke weed to maintain. I just fucking couldn't. I really wished I could. I saw other people who could, who were survivors but who weren't quite as indisputably fucked out of their tree, who could hold down a job and a social life.

But instead, I had a shitty, perfect apartment all my own. Dandelions turning into medicine in a jar. One pair of pants. Unanswered letters in a box. An old computer with some poems on it. A plum-colored futon that I slept on for seventeen hours a day. Some solo, silent hoodie walks when I could get off of it.

When I was a kid, I remember thinking: *If you're this fucked-up, either you fix it early, or it just gets papered over.*

I dove.

Lay on that futon.

I rebuilt the structure of the building from the cellular level. And I healed. I healed true.

22. Psychiatric Survivor Movement

The psychiatric survivor movement saved my life, and it was the secret reason I came to Toronto. There is a radical crazy person movement there, along with the South Asians and Sri Lankans and mixed girls and queers of color. Some of us are in both movements.

I'd heard rumors of it. I read reviews about zines that talked about mental illness, and I would write away for them, send my two stamps and a dollar, and I would read those zines—*Fantastic Fanzine* and *I Am Good Inside* and *Construction Paper*—the most. Those riot grrrl zines with brilliant sixteen- and twenty-one-year old girls' handwritten stories about the goriest incest and ritual abuse stuff you could imagine. And I might've been years away from being able to talk about it in a coherent sentence, but inside, I was like, *I need this.* I was pretty sure my mind was pretty different, in the way my mother's had been. It was about being an abuse survivor, but it was also about having Severe Generalized Depression so bad I'd spent my seventh-grade summer vacation wanting to kill myself—I mean every damn day—and not talking about it. Or about my first year of college, after accidentally smoking a joint with angel dust in it, when I was at high school graduation, so dissociated that all of the world looked unreal, like a giant TV program, and not being able to talk about it. Losing the ability to talk. Being pre-verbal and too weird for regular human company.

The big fear I had was that I'd go crazy like my mom, but worse. I feared not even being able to pass enough to hold down a job. I'd fall into that pit in the floor that waits for folks who are too fucked-up by our families and the world to be able to look normal on the street, to be able to maintain enough to work a coffee shop job. And I'd never come out.

But the psych survivor movement had been hard for me to find til then. One of the first people to show up to an early *Prison News Service* meeting was Don Weitz. Everyone seemed to know him. Don was like an energetic Pez dispenser; a five-foot-two, balding, white-haired, anti-Zionist, Jewish grandpa. Don's parents had institutionalized him after he dropped out of Dartmouth in 1951. The doctors had given him insulin shock. He'd gotten out, been radicalized by the '60s, and helped to start the Canadian mental patients liberation movement. Don always made sure that *Bulldozer* had tons of madness content, with an analysis, not always found in prison justice papers, that psych institutions and prisons were related, and we connected the struggles against ableism and for prison justice.

Parkdale was Toronto's biggest psychiatric ghetto, with thou-sands of people living in boarding houses. If a patient was dis-charged from the Queen Street Mental Health Centre or the Clarke Institute, you'd get general welfare and a daily living allowance and could live with a bunch of other nuts in a house with bad food. At the hulking fortress that was the Queen Street Mental Health Centre there was a wall that had been built by unpaid crazy person labor to block it off from the rest of the west-side neighborhood. Parkdale had once been a pretty village of Victorian homes, separated from the hoi polloi, until the 1950s and '60s when the Victorians were divided into tiny bachelor apartments, and the second generation (but maybe first on record) of West Indians, Sri Lankans, and refugees had moved into poor people apartments at Jameson, Westmoreland. At the same time, the '60s de-institutionalization scheme and new meds had made it possible to release crazy folks from the bin into group homes, and they could be found sitting, drinking coffee, and smoking cigs all over Queen Street.

And out of that, sometimes, there was insurrection. The psych survivor movement in Toronto started out of that perfect storm of crazy, brown, and queer people who lived together in Parkdale. People who'd started to organize inside boarding homes. Every year, there were protests outside Queen Street Mental Health or the Clarke Institute on College Street against electroshock or forced treatment. There was an annual Psychiatric Survivor Pride Day, a day or a weekend full of healing ceremonies and really good, free food for nuts, of workshops and performances and protests organized out of the psych survivor legal worker office of Parkdale Community Legal Services. Sometimes, there would be a whole bunch of nuts walking up Queen Street with a bullhorn, holding up cheap posterboard signs that read HOMES NOT HOVELS and NO FORCED TREATMENT. Yelling against community treatment orders that meant the cops could come get you if you started trying to wean off your dose and you flunked your weekly piss test. Or when a boarding house burned down because of how disgusting the conditions were.

Sometimes, there was just the exhale I felt walking west of Ossington. The exhale that I, too, could be brown and nuts on the street, and no one would stare at me that hard. I could be at Coffee Time eating a coconut donut or sitting at the scarred wood tables in the West Indian and Black Heritage Collection at the Parkdale Library, reading small-press editions of Ahdri Zina Mandiela and other Sister Vision Press poems and the broken-spined, often-checked-out copy of *This Bridge Called My Back*—and feel myself surrounded by radical crazies, brown people, queers, and those who were all of the above. (Also, the Parkdale branch had the Toronto Public Library's one VHS copy of *Born in Flames.*)

I hadn't been drugged or shocked or locked up, but I lived my life constantly worried that I would be. I just hadn't been caught yet. I was like the others, even if I wasn't in the psych hospital.

The protests were important. But what was even more important to me was the compassion. Just the room to be crazy. I remember meeting with the Psych Survivor Pride Day crew in the back of The Meeting Place homeless drop-in, everyone wigging out at once, and Don and Graeme smiling. Rafael and I would look at each other and start to sing the Herbie Hancock song we'd been into lately, the one that sounded like bird calls. Everyone just smiled at us.

23. Punk Desi Girls

Amina. Vashti. Anjali. Leila. Sharmini.

You were the weird, queer brown girls who made me move here. You were the weird, queer brown girls who showed me how to be brown, all the ways there were to be a South Asian girl.

Booze can, red lights in the basement, another after-hours benefit for *Prison News Service* at the South Africa Center in Kensington Market, 1996. Anjali danced in a flannel over a thermal, shaved head dyed green growing in, the dye half washed out, giving her hair that look like mold was growing in it that green dye gives you when it washes out. Dancing in her plaid shirt over hoodie over thermal and jeans, still femme, delicate, jumping up on the table and shimmying to Biggie singing "Mo Money Mo Problems." I went up to her and started raving, South Asian this South Asian that, and she was like, "Oh, do you identify as a South Asian?" Not hostile, just asking.

Anjali hung out with Gordon and what's-her-name who never talked, bald-headed and silent. They hung in a tight pack of twenty-one-year-old roommate queer kids who had all run away. Years later, I saw Anjali at 52 Inc, gyrating wildly and drunkenly on a tiny table top, a $134 tequila bill waiting for her.

That night, she cornered me in the bathroom, screaming at me, "I just want to know, sometimes you smile at me, sometimes you don't! What's up with that?" She was dramalicious; one of the ones you needed most, who maybe needed you the most. Why were they always like that?

Amina was fat, beautifully fat, like the sexiest hippo you'd ever seen, with that gap between her front teeth, and her magnificent breasts, and her headwraps worn over her crinkly hair. Radwa, her girlfriend, was short and skinny and had a rooster boy haircut, little wire glasses, and nutmeg-brown skin. They were hot like fuck together. And together they ran the desi music show that all of the city's desis listened to, Masala Mix, from the community radio station in the basement of Ryerson University, that had its mics and headphones held together with duct tape, and they talked about domestic violence and desi gays in 1996 because they had a captive audience; in 1996, there was no other place to hear desi music.

Amina looked like a vision of something different. She was brown and femme, rocking ice-cream white pantsuits and bejeweled chappals, the hottest, shiny, magenta shalwars tight across her breasts. She said that word, "femme," and she was a desi from somewhere else, just like me. She was going to law school. Amina talked about being molested, and wrote erotica. I wanted to grow up to be just like her—shining, behind the turntables, creating a whole community—a bad-ass brown girl thriving despite the cold.

The first time I saw Leila, I caught my breath at her phenotype. I knew some folks thought she was white, but me, I could read her question. Her eyes were mestiza hazel, big old beautiful cow eyes, her nose just like my dad's, that exact half-white, half-brown shade of skin. Ecru. She was a raver and she danced all night at all the best and most famous clubs and threw her head back and laughed and was vulnerable behind it all. Had a white, working-class Northern Ontario mum and an Indo-Guyanese dad and reminded me so much of myself I didn't even know how to say it in words. When I saw her at Krishantha's poetry launch in the community room of the St. James Town housing projects, I walked up to her and said abruptly, "Are you Burgher?" and she said, "No," and I said, "I am. Okay then," and moved away to sit with Rafael. She teased me about it for years after, about how shitty and awkward my social skills were in that moment. I knew. I was okay with her teasing. I was desperate to find kin, and awkward. But the point was, we recognized each other. Kept recognizing each other.

Sharmini was another one who could pass. Or not. Who was looking? Who determined who could pass and who couldn't? Was it not being visible? Or was it how people knew how to see? Sharmini was creamy too, with hazel eyes, one curl quirked over her eye. She was a raver, and she had one curl quirked over her eye, and she was lovers with Vishnu, this tamarind bean-pod Trini queer boy.

You girls, you showed me. Walking through Kensington Market and Parkdale, so many shades of brown, and there was one that called my name.

24. Funkasia, 1999

When I got a little less sick, or could fake being able-bodied for a minute, I went to Funkasia. That was when I lived in a basement apartment at Davenport and Shaw for $450 a month, which got half an hour of natural light a day, so I burned out lightbulbs every two weeks, but it was mine, all mine, I had a door that shut and locked, and o, that was sweet. I didn't have a proper winter coat, but wore a leather jacket and five hoodies and thermals and a Thinsulate-lined watch cap and matching gloves—and still called myself femme, because I was. I could barely afford the bus, but I had a junker adult trike that I called Babygirl. I would hit the Davenport bike lane that got me to Church and Wellesley in fifteen minutes, pedaling standing up, skirt flapping in the wind, and I would meet my friends at the Red Spot, a club on Church Street.

The Red Spot was owned by Tamils, and it was up a narrow, shitty, flight of stairs, the air thick with cigarette smoke from lots of Players and Belmont Extra Milds. This was where the queer open mic, Clit Lit, and the benefits for the Queer Caribbean float in Pride and Women of Color against Police Brutality happened. And on the third Sunday of each month, we went up the stairs to Funkasia.

The lime-green flyer pronounced BHANGRA SOCA TAMIL FILM HINDI FILM DANCEHALL HIPHOP and had a picture of a punk girl with a nose ring and big eyebrows. This is a queer positive space, haters stay home. And everybody who was in there was South Asian and queer or somebody's straight and supportive cousin, and if you went after 10:30 p.m., the line was around the freaking block. You would wait there til 1:30 a.m., half an hour before last call, to get in and dance your ass off hard for a half hour, a half hour of the best, hungriest, most-needed bliss.

And I was scared as hell to go. I was a shivering, little mixed-race brown girl on a starvation diet who had barely two pairs of pants to her name and wore round John Lennonesque glasses acquired in 1994 at a LensCrafters that I was super embarrassed about but had no money to replace. And I feared the gauntlet of late-'90s identity politics like I feared being pulled aside by Immigration at the border or having to walk home from Church and Wellesley to Davenport and Shaw in the middle of winter if I had a flat.

On the street, I was uncomfortably light brown, but brown enough. People knew I was something even if they didn't know what that something was. But in Desh Pardesh and Funkasia, there were always some bitchy Punjabi girls from Scarbs or 'sauga or Brampton who'd say to me, with a tinkling laugh, "Oh, I was wondering why you were here ... I never would've been able to tell!" *Mean Girls* had nothing on second-generation desis whose parents gave them shit for being too Canadian and who wanted to be more down than somebody.

But I had some friends—Keisha who was Black and desi from Trinidad, Idil who was Somali and Egyptian, Gita who was Tamil and Sinhalese and Burgher, Shezad who was Tamil but as light as me—and we would troop up those damn stairs to the Red Spot and writhe around in the smoke.

It was there, in the Red Spot, that I found my brown. There and in the Market, before everything changed, and while shopping in Parkdale for curry leaf and giant bags of Lankan tea or buying gulab jamuns for makeshift Diwalis. Here there was a whole mess of diaspora, all slammed in together. The Red Spot was the only club that played our music, and we had to get along, or at least pretend to. Guju punk girls with shaved heads growing in green, sexy aunties in red shalwars smoking cigars and staring at you (and you could imagine how their bangles would jangle as they fisted you), Trini desi butches with rooster boy haircuts and lungis, arts administrators trying to dance off the stress. Here were all kinds of desis who hated each other, maybe had invaded each other's countries, hacked off each other's heads back home, and whose families had lost everything when they moved to freezing immigrant apartments in St. James Town or King Street.

But here, we were all shivering through Immigration, doing cab driver and dishwasher jobs and going to George Brown college, and we sort of, kind of, got along. I didn't know that I could say, "I don't know how to do bhangra. My mom is white, and my dad was so angry about where we came from that he never said shit, and anyway, I'm Sri Lankan, not Punjabi." I just stared at the moves and memorized them as fast as I could. I realized that bhangra moves are just passive aggression—come here, come here. Go away, go away.

TAMIL FILM HINDI FILM *SHOLAY KUCH KUCH HOTA HAI.* DJ Jitin's remixes of Lauryn Hill and the Fugees. Six degrees of separation mixes: Talvin Singh and Asian Dub Foundation's "Free Satpal Ram" and "Naxalite," Badmarsh & Shri and State of Bengal and all the others whose names I can't remember without Google now. Whining songs of desire that curved my waist brown and sweet like tea, sour and salt like tamarind balls crusted with raw sugar. Dancehall that felt more comfortable because of this half-assed, not complicated enough dream that the Caribbean was so mixed that somehow I fit in. I worried that punk rock had ruined my sense of rhythm, but I danced and breathed and felt my hips hurt and stared at people and stayed out late. And somewhere in that sweaty brown hot box of brown gay, I found myself.

All three of the sisters wore long 1930s dresses, European meets subcontinent meets island. The photo is sepia, like their skin. All three of the girls have their hair trimmed into bobs. No one is smiling but Cristabel, who looks hopeful, like *C'mon guys, it's not that bad!* My grandmother, Jackie, stares the camera down, unsmiling. So does Renee, the darkest one of all except for my great-grandfather.

I picked that one. Slipped it out of its frame and slid it under my armpit. No one would notice, not for a while, that these ancestors are gone from that neglected corner of the bookshelf. I slip them under the mattress. I am stealing my ancestors. They will come with me to Toronto.

25. Dad Again

When I came out to my dad, I was twenty-one and about to leave forever. We were in the basement, where he always was. Old brown couch I used to jump on when I was six with all the kids from the block. All the lights out, a tumbler of Johnnie Walker Red by his right hand. That's what he did on the weekends. Can't touch scotch now, or can but don't want to, because while I am my father's daughter in many ways, there are many ways I don't want to be just like him. He was Johnnie Walker, the History Channel on low, and staying up til four a.m., when he finally passed out, then getting up at six to catch the early commuter rail into Boston for work.

I wasn't planning to have the big queer conversation with him. I was actually trying to have an awkward as hell conversation about me getting married to Rafael so I could stay in Canada. I figured in this way he would understand; we'd switched countries so many times in so many sketchy ways that it was almost a family tradition.

I remember him saying, "But what if you want to do something that Rafael doesn't want you to do?" I remember telling him that it was for the papers, that both of us were queer, and

I remember him saying in the dark, "Well, what do you think I did before I married your mother?"

In the hostels? In London where he lived with his super-best, super-pretty friend, David from Trinidad, for years before he met my mother?

"You do whatever you want. You just get married."

I let the silence be after that. I knew there could be no further conversation. But my dad had just told me that, in proud Sri Lankan tradition, he had got it on with men.

Before I left, I found my dad's porn stash. In the attic, I was trying to figure out everything I would take with me because this was my last chance. I had already snuck my birth certificate, social security card, and passport out of my mother's locked filing cabinet after searching for the key for the hour she was out at the supermarket. I was picking which books, which photographs, which childhood things I could pack with me in the van. What I could get away with taking and absolutely needed. I saw a pile of books in the corner that was instantly recognizable: the covers of *Best American Erotica* anthologies, *On a Bed of Rice*, that first Asian-American collection with the terrible name, and all that mid-'90s porn revolution, tasteful kinky shit you could find in a Borders. *Shit, those aren't mine. Shit, those have my dad's name written in the front.*

My dad was a pretty, pretty man. In his youth, a skinny, brown elegant boy, tall and long with big, deep eyes, skin the color of tobacco leather, and thick straight black jute hair, all angles and long legs. Now he was middle-aged and going silver, with more sad lines around his eyes and mouth, still mournful

and fine. When we went to Provincetown for day trips summer, he'd still get hit on constantly. He'd act like he it, but he'd walk ahead of my mother and me, strolling, behind his back. Was he remembering Galle Face Green, Lankan park, or the beach near Kuala Lumpur? Was he re bering a different sun, browner men, the train tracks b Bambalapitiya station, cock in mouth, on his knees, 1965

If Freud is right at all and anything other than an ass guess it makes sense that my father's daughter grew up and love brown, faggot sexy-ass men of any gender of qu

On a white painted shelf in their living room, posi among my dad's model soldiers, were some of his famil tographs. Dad had objected to them being displayed, mother had overrode him. So there they all were, the taken during his first visit to see his family in years, visit, in 1989. Tall and uncomfortable-looking, he posed his parents, who were brown and wrinkled, shorter and coming up to his shoulders. And the older ones, the sepia, the ones my grandmother had brought with her big brown leather albums when she and my grandfather the last boat out of Kuala Lumpur in 1942 when the Ja invaded, were the only things they had taken with them. left behind their middle-class Ceylonese life—the house one helping with the cooking, engineer/teacher life—w these two big books of family photographs.

There was one portrait of Grandma and her two Renee and Cristabel, and their little brother, Lawrenc ning and spoiled, the son they'd kept having kids til th

26. Not Picking Up the Phone

My dad always avoided letters from home. Like, always. They were those thin blue aerogram letters that immigrant kids remember their far-off families sending in the '80s. This was before phone cards, email, or Gmail chat when plane tickets were expensive and long-distance phone calls cost sixty cents a minute. Those aerogram letters were thin enough to take flight all the way from Australia, India, Mexico, or Somali. And there was only a page to write on them, so you could only say the most important things. The kind of things that could be written in a small space. The most polite things.

They would arrive and be carried into the kitchen to our robin's egg blue Formica countertop, where my father would ignore them for months.

My mother would yell at him, "Justin, you have to open the letters!" and he'd grunt and say, "Helen," and duck his chin, grimace, and walk away, probably to the basement. The relatives would call too, and then it'd be, "Justin, you have to call them back!"

But it was always so easy for my dad to avoid phone calls. There was a crazy time difference, so there was only like two hours when they both were awake, and it was easy to just be a little late that day. It was sixty-nine cents a minute so he could only talk for ten. Massachusetts is about as far away on the planet as you can get from Melbourne.

Even though they acted like it just happened, it was no accident that my father ended up here. He did not want to be near his family. I mean, not only was he the dark one who lived after the light-skinned one died, but he didn't graduate from high school and there were rumors of faggotry and then he married some white woman who didn't have any money and moved to America with her.

So there was a family tradition of not picking up the phone, answering letters, or calling back. You can live a whole life not looking at what you don't know how to deal with.

So when the phone rang, those three short rings that said it was an international call, I didn't pick up. I sat in the corner and stared at it til it stopped. I 33-7d the messages so I didn't have to listen. I was still running.

I knew how. It was diaspora and escape, in my epigenetics.

27. Learning to Be Brown, Parts 1–3

Part 1:

I don't know how to write about becoming brown, but I know I have to.

Learning to be brown is a process some of us go through. Most of us don't talk about it. We shut the fuck up, study up, and pass into brownness as fast as we can. We don't want to admit our dorky inauthentic, mixed-race roots. We are fragile. We are making up for lost time. People already laugh at us mixed-race kids because we look weird; they're going to laugh harder if we admit what we don't know, what we were never taught by parents who were trying to survive by assimilating into whiteness, or at least not being noticed, as fast as possible. We have to get it back, get it all back.

In *The Courage to Heal*, it says that if your family didn't teach you certain things, like how to make friends, or have boundaries, it's not your fault. You just have to learn in adulthood, instead of flailing and freaking out and hating yourself because you don't know how to do it. I think that's true about being Black or brown, too, if you grew up with folks who didn't teach your food or language or what to do with all that hair.

When I was twenty-two, I was that kind of awkward mixed kid who drags themselves over a bed of nails and self-loathing on a daily basis. I didn't know anything, or so I thought. *I don't know anything, I don't know anything*, I repeated. I cringed. I thought I was a fake. I was the most terrible, inauthentic brown person ever.

So I watched and I studied. I silently faked it at queer bhangra parties instead of knowing that I could ask how to do the moves, because, of course, I hadn't grown up going to Punjabi weddings. I felt lost, hanging out with the first radical South Asians I ever met, Indians from the north who'd grown up in Toronto. They were bonding by imitating their parents' accents the way second-generation kids do, and I couldn't join in when they smiled at me inquisitively, expectantly. My dad had an accent, but it was a Sri Lankan British accent, not this one.

When your dad is the Black or brown one, most likely he never learned how to cook, so he can't teach you the recipes. I found *Leith's Sri Lankan Cookery* and *Fire and Spice* in the library. I figured out how to make thosai from Strictly Bulk rice flour and urad dhal and discovered that it is a bitch to get any rice-based pancake to ferment when you live in Toronto, not a warm, tropical country. I nerved myself up to go into Kana SuperSave to buy curry leaf, worried I would face cross-examination. I would do all kinds of Jedi mind tricks on myself: *I'm North Indian, I'm Afghani, and I need these curry leaves. That's why I'm light. That's why I'm in here.*

But often, what was also true was that I blended in, in Toronto. That was the balm. If you could be any kind of dark-brown curly haired, olive-skinned girl in New York, then in

Toronto you could be any kind of light-brown kid in a hoodie going into a small Sri Lankan grocery in Parkdale or walking down Bloor and Lansdowne.

The first time I go to a Sri Lankan restaurant, it's the Araani on Spadina, nestled between Chinese, Vietnamese, and Caribbean restaurants in a way that shouted pan-Asian solidarity, in a community that is the same. It's still a shock when I see the words "Sri Lankan" written in public. Sri Lanka feels like a secret, folded up tight, light-brown and dusty, a crackled piece of old paper shoved away in an attic box. I have to breathe hard not to have a panic attack. How do I talk about this totally naked shame feeling of going to a restaurant run by people in my community for the first time at age twenty-two. My father didn't know how to cook—he was a boy—and like many Sri Lankans in the US, we either grew up in small communities like Lancaster ("Sri Lankaster") California, or Staten Island, or we grew up isolated.

But in Toronto, the words "Sri Lankan" were everywhere: on tiny storefront Sri Lankan/West Indian/East Indian/Canadian Groceries whose boxes spilled out eggplants and okra, where fresh mint and curry leaves were found in ziplock bags in the fridge. There was a Sri Lankan Worker's Action Centre, and every day I walked past a Tamil housing co-op at Bloor and Lansdowne where the same words were spelled out in Sinhalese and Tamil, or just Tamil. When you said "Sri Lanka," people in Toronto knew where you meant. Sri Lanka was the girl they grew up with, another Toronto ethnicity that went to school with you at York Collegiate or Central Tech, or that kid down the hall's parents. The States only let in the rich Sri Lankans after the riots in 1983; Canada had a more generous refugee and immigration policy, and Little Jaffna in the Scar (Scarborough) has the largest Sri Lankan population off the island. In the 1980s, Toronto had many mixed-race and mixed-income neighborhoods filled with kids whose parents had come from recently decolonized countries. Rafael told me that when the Fugees came to Toronto in 1995 and yelled, "If you're a refugee in the building, put your hands up!" they were shocked when the whole house threw their hands up.

Toronto has so many ways of being brown and being South Asian. Ten percent of the city is South Asian, and when they say South Asian, they don't mean Indian. They mean Indo-Trini, Malayali, Sri Lankan, Bengali, desi from South Africa, and half-and-half. Half is kind of a cultural identity. South Asian with a white mom. *She's not white, she's mixed. Bi-racial. I know she looks white, but she's mixed. I have to ask you a question ... are you mixed? I knew it! I couldn't tell what you were. Mixed people are so beautiful! Oh. You're the best of both worlds, huh. Oh. You must be confused.*

When I walk down the street in Kensington in the warm sunshine, past those boxes of cheap vegetables and fruit, the Arab desi Trini Gutamalteco groceries, the egg store and the bike shack, warm sun on my shoulders, I get passed by all kinds of brown. Brown that feels miles closer to my kind of brown than New York brown. In New York, I spent hours walking the streets, staring at the brown girls of New York with light tan skin, smooth, like a brown egg, café con leche, or dark like toasted coconut. Light tan with freckles. New York was a city of girls with brown curly hair, olive, light brown, medium brown, dark brown, golden skin. Even the white girls were brunettes, stressed out, holding a paper coffee cup and a briefcase and a Century 21 shopping bag on the N train. But my country's name was a secret there, a secret I didn't know how to tell. Sometimes people would begin to speak. A squint, a smile, an extension of Spanish to me, then a pull-back when I said, "No, sorry, *poquito, no mas.*" I didn't know how to say where I was from, and when I met the rare other South Asian, they were full blooded, so Indian, so from Queens or New Jersey, so Punjabi, and my half Sri Lankan feels so weird.

Sometimes when I walked into a Sri Lankan grocery store in Toronto, I couldn't stand the scrutiny. I was too naked to deal with even the most well-meaning, sweet questions. But sometimes they don't come. Sometimes, there is the question and then the *huh*, understanding, because there are women on the island who look just like me. But there is also, "Miss, you are Indian? You are Sri Lankan?" Somebody fucked somebody who shouldn't have fucked somebody, and here you are, a remnant of that fucking. I had to get my nerve together to step into that shop for fish cutlets or samosas or Jaffna curry powder in a big bag, red rice, eggplants, and pickle.

When I did, I scarfed them down in the bright white Canadian winter sunlight, greasy and crisp, musky with the taste of back home and delicious.

Part 2:

When I moved to Toronto, I worked on my thesis long distance. It was about mixed-race Sri Lankan women's identity formation and organizing from colonization to the present day. I got a community library card at Robarts, the big tower library at the University of Toronto, and would curl up in a cubby there for hours, reading. All the books I needed had been stolen from the Brooklyn Public Library, or they didn't have them. They had them here, even the old ones, *Ceylon and the Hollanders: 1658-1796, Ceylon and the Portuguese: 1505-1658*, narrow, blue, hardbound, telling the stories of colonization. Sri Lanka had gotten it three times: from the Portuguese, the Dutch, and the British, and then after independence, we'd gotten it again from the World Bank. I looked up my last name in the indexes of these books, and there it was. I looked down a little bit and read "See: Samarasinha." It was there as a cross-reference. I stared at it for a while.

I had been staring at all the names that sounded vaguely European in Kumari Jayawardena's *Feminism and Nationalism in the Third World*'s Sri Lankan chapter—especially at all the de Alwises, de Silvas, Hoffmans, and Fernandos—and wondering if they were mixed like me, or mixed like my dad, or mixed a little bit, or just Christian. There were charts that showed how Burghers were accepted as Burghers if they spoke English, had a European last name, and went to church—and Eurasians usually had a brown dad, and weren't accepted into the Burgher societies. And then their were the Kaffirs and Caliscos, descendants of enslaved East Africans brought to Sri Lanka from Somalia, who were barely a whisper, like the Veddahs, the indigenous people.

Here was what my name maybe had been before the marriages briefly mentioned between Sri Lankan women and all the Portuguese and Dutch men—soldiers who didn't bring their wives with them on the ships. "Marriages." Not rapes. Of course.

I read Vijay Prashad, *The Karma of Brown Folk*, found Indran Amirthanayagam's *The Elephants of Reckoning*. Rafael and I read *Dalit: The Black Untouchables of India* and chewed over whether Dravidian folks were of African descent, and if all of South Asia's conflicts could be broken down into an Aryan-Dravidian conflict or whether that was wishful thinking and it was a little more complicated. I read *Dragon Ladies: Asian American Feminists Breathe Fire* and all the new anthologies— it seemed like there was a new one every week—*Plural Desires: Writing Bisexual Women's Realities*, with all the women of color in it, and *The Very Inside: An Anthology of Writings by Asian & Pacific Islander Lesbians*, and *Piece of My Heart: A Lesbian of Color Anthology*. It was a woman-of-color vision with lots of mixed girls. Lots of girls who had been colonized by Britain— the Hong Kong girls and Malaysian girls and the Trinidadian girls—we had a Commonwealth connection. Countries where there was mixing and British accents, and varied Black and brown children.

"You should meet Krisantha," Rafael had said, a bunch of people had told me. Krisantha was this Sri Lankan poet, Sinhalese but down; he'd come to Canada in the 1960s. He wrote epic poems and performed them. I didn't really like his second book, but it was amazing that he existed, a Sri Lankan radical poet writing in English. I really did like his poem, "Aay, wha' kinda Indian arr u?" I bought it on cassette from the Sri Lankan restaurant where activists like us hung out after close-talking shit, or from his P.O. box, and we played it, or sections of it, on CKLN constantly.

When I met Krisantha, he looked at me like I reminded him of something he'd rather not be reminded of. His niece, Sumaya, was about my color, but she looked like a Bollywood model, straight hair with a little wave, creamy skin, and big eyes. She was pretty and acceptable in a way I wasn't. Someone told me, "Oh, yeah, there's totally Burgher in that family but they don't like to talk about it."

I introduced myself, spluttering, talking about my thesis, saying that I was Sri Lankan and a poet. He didn't smile. "Michael Ondaatje, you should read him. He's your people," he said and walked off. I was stunned, standing there with my hand out. It was the ultimate diss. I didn't want to read Michael Ondaatje. All I knew was that he was that famous Burgher guy who everyone sneered at. He'd just rediscovered that he wasn't white. When I read *Running in the Family*, his memoir, I got guiltily swept away in the fever dream of it, the weird auntie and the drinking and the assertion, when one of the characters was asked what ethnicity he was, "God alone knows, sir."

On the other hand, Amuthan waited tables at 52 Inc, the cafe/bar with spoken word and DJ nights run by two white women that was filled with downtown queer Black and brown bohemia. His slick tamarind brownness, shaved head, and smooth muscles were incongruent next to so many vegan white-girls in lavender-cotton sack dresses, so much restrained Canadian good taste.

When I danced with Amuthan, he just swooped up without question, put his hands on my waist, and started to move me around the tiny dance floor, dancing salsa, holding my waist and moving me. He tried to talk Spanish to me and just assumed I was Latina—Bolivian or Chilean like Ernesto or Rafael. When I said I was Lankan, he froze up.

"You are?" He got real quiet. We danced for a while, in silence. Two step, two step.

Then he said, "Kumaran and them, they like to talk about how great the village is. I'm from the village. I had one pair of pants and one shirt. I never slept on a mattress before I came here. They were in the JVP[1], and they like to talk about how great it would be if we all went back to the village, but they had servants all their life. They don't know what it's like." Amuthan had been arrested and taken to Boosa, the Sri Lankan prison and torture center where so many people were rounded up. They'd locked him up for a year and broken his ankles. But now

---

1 For the approximately 98.2 percent with no knowledge of Sri Lankan history: the JVP, or Janath—Vimukthi Peramu—was a working-class Sinhalese Marxist-Leninist style political movement / paramilitary organization that talked about decoloniality. Some of the more urban middle-class members were really excited about going "back to the land / the village" and scraping off colonial mentality, as you can see in the above conversation. They created two armed uprisings against the ruling government in 1971 and 1987–89, and decided to get into government and become a political party. Shit is as buckwild with them as it is with any other part of Sri Lankan politics. People had hope that the JVP would be liberatory, but they were pretty into the war and pretty into Sinhalese chauvinism.

somehow he was here, looking beautiful and brown and dis-
trustful. He avoided me after that, gave me a cautious nod and
looked away. He didn't want any part of any of that.

Part 3:

When Keisha and Idil and I got together for Diwali, we cooked
all the food we knew how to. Chicken from the Portuguese
butcher in the Market who had cheap free-range legs, big
bunches of collards that were as green as we could find in
December in Toronto, sweet potatoes, white potatoes to throw
into the chicken curry from the twenty-pound bag I had in the
back porch, and dhal, a.k.a. parripu. Idil came along for the ride,
even though she was Somali and Egyptian, not South Asian.
We'd joke and talk. I'd heard whispers that the reason why some
Tamils were so dark and had loose crinkled hair that looked
East African was that Somalis and Ethiopians would trade with
us. We'd married each other. I don't remember who said it on
the streets of Kensington, but somebody did: that Ceylon, Sri
Lanka's old name, meant "the lost boat," and it meant the boat
the Somalis and Ethiopians had sent out that didn't come back.
Me and Rafael had had that book *Dalit: The Black Untouchables
of India*, that talked about the Afro-diasporic connections to
Dravidian culture, and it was right next to the *Black History
for Beginners* book that talked about how Pacific Islanders in
Papua New Guinea and Aboriginal folks in Australia were really
Black. Was that why my hair was curly? It got trippy; if I was light
brown but really oppressed because South Indians/Dravidians

were really African diasporic and working class, then maybe I was more oppressed than the snooty Punjabi girls? Maybe all the fights in Desh came down to a privileged Aryan northern Indian versus oppressed Southern Indian dynamic?

Mostly I tried to hang out in the muttering corners, with the other race rejects. Sometimes, I fell asleep inside a circle of books.

Some nights, before I fell asleep, I stared at the sepia portrait I'd stolen. *Grandma, I reach back to you. Back through the brown ink of your face. What was your life like?*

28. Changed My Name

wrong is not yours

for all of us with beautiful long names from the homelands,
especially those of us who got them in adulthood.

one day you are a 22-year-old with dreadlocked half-desi hair
you decided to lock when you did double dip mescaline on new
year's eve after staring at pictures of sadhus in south india.
years before Carol's Daughter or Palmer coconut hair milk or
Kinky Curly in Target and you have no idea what to do with all
that curly curly hair

who decides you wants to change her name from albrecht no
more albrecht   you want your great-grandmothers   you
are a 22-year-old on a straight diet of frantz fanon marlon riggs
and chrystos   you are a sri lankan christian daughter of the
dutch east india   company you want no more albrecht no more
rape in your pelvis no more *where'd you get that name* no more
are you adopted no more

even through yr grandmas whisper   *keep a white name*
for the passport   keep as many passports as possible   you
never know what boat you're going to have to get on   who
you'll have to bullshit in an immigration office
you never know where we'll have to run to   make home in
sip your tea   cook your rice   wait for death
looking at an ocean that almost looks like yours

but you want your great-grandmother's name who means hot
pepper   who walked out of the galicia with 13 children
your other great-grandmother whose name is a footnote in a
lankan history book's cross-referenced index you find researching
yr senior thesis on mixed-race women in sri lanka   teachers
union organizers and sluts everyone of us
and you get something infinitely googleable and infinitely unpro-
nounceable except for ukrainians and lankans and dravidians

and even when dennis kucinich runs for president
and puts an mp3 file on his website saying how to say his name
and you think it might be a good idea too
your name is not wrong
wrong is not your name
it is your own
your own

your own

your own
your own

My grandmother, whom I never met (that I can remember), taught me subconsciously and psychically and across the waters and time to have as many names, identities, and passports as possible.

On hand.
Just in case.

Because you never know where you might end up or where you might have to get to. Or who you might have to turn yourself into, in order to be safe.

I change my name when I am twenty-two. I am sick of being looked askance at. I don't look like an Albrecht. *Are you adopted. Or what? Oh, really? Alvarez? What is it?* I change my name, but I keep my legal name legal, the Dutch colonial Dutch East India Company name on my passport and driver's license so I can blink hard and look like the immigration guy's hot Italian, mixed-something daughter. I play it all ways, to pass. To get across the border. Any border. I am trying to be responsible and also respect what my grandma told me. I still want to have an ace in the hole. Sometimes, I want to be Lankan with my colonial Lankan, stupid, old-school European name that is more Lankan that trying to go back in a footnote to before the predators came.

And sometimes, in the back of my head, like a secret thing that I write really small and paint over with dark red paint right after, I want to find my family. And this is the name I will use to do it.

29. Landed

When you apply for Canadian Immigration through marriage, your sponsor has to sign an undertaking that they are fiscally responsible for you for the next ten years. You can't go on welfare. You can't really collect family benefits or disability. It's a way the government makes sure immigrants don't get to use any of the lovely Canadian social safety net that our taxes pay for. A lot of husbands who sponsor their wives tell them that that means they can't get divorced, that if they try to leave their marriages, they'll be deported. There's a law that makes that illegal, but the system doesn't always pay attention to it, and the women don't always know.

When Rafael signs the form, I know it is a problem, but I also don't have an alternative.

I got the form in my hand. Remembered Rafael's mother Paula's knowing look, her saying, when I told her how broke we were and how hard it was being off the books, "But, you know, it won't always be that way." Her remembering when she was just like us — one-room apartment, roaches. And here it was, that day. The day when I would get my landed immigrant status, it was true: things were no longer quite so hard. When I would get an Ontario Health Insurance card, a Social Insurance Number, the ability to rise out of the basement to that world I'd been looking at through a smeared, ground-level window.

On the day I was supposed to report to the big immigration center, at the farthest reach of the subway into the immigrant suburb of Etobicoke, there was a transit strike. I called the 800 number. I thought about the 800 numbers I had memorized— the Assaulted Women's Helpline, the Toronto Rape Crisis Centre, the tenant hotline. I told them, "I can't make it to my appointment. The subway's on strike."

Deep sigh. "Fine. Just wait. We'll give you another date."

When the postcard with the date and time showed up, I got an early start, dressed in my least patched-up best, and took the subway, making sure that I got there on time, right at eight a.m. The waiting room was that diarrhea yellow of all institutional waiting rooms, filled with folks who looked just like some variation of me, all the folks who'd stood in that long-ass immigration and citizenship line at Dundas and University, before they moved their offices somewhere further out in the suburbs so people didn't have to see us. The ones who had finally made it, waiting.

When my name was called, I walked up to the lady with a beehive hairdo who looked like Anne Murray. She looked at my forms and then at me. She handed me a long, pale piss-yellow form through the slot.

It said Family Class Landed Immigrant Status on it.

"This is the wrong one," I said.

"What do you mean, dear?"

"It's supposed to be compassionate and humanitarian. My partner, um, husband, he was abusive. I submitted all the forms."

"I don't see anything about that." She paused. Probably thought she was doing me a favor. She leaned in, lowered her voice. "Don't break up a marriage over something like that. All I know is, you have this card now. I should give it to you, shouldn't I?"

BAM! Stamp on the passport. Coveted, coveted document stapled into coveted, coveted passport. "Take the elevator downstairs. You can get your SIN number and OHIP application there."

I was silent. I'd passed through. But what now?

Part Four

OPENING / FEMME LIKE A FIST

"We run like the answer to ancestors' questions."

—*Gabriel Teodros*

30. Early '90s New York Femme Memory No. 2

When I was nineteen, I used to take hours to dress up. The red vintage garter belt I'd found at the vintage shop called Love Saves the Day, my basic black mini from the sale table of the Boston Urban Outfitters, my Docs, thigh-highs from Marshall's, my basic black tank top. I would put on makeup for hours, fucking up and enjoying the ritual, my hands shaking, making the liquid eyeliner blur. I would jerk off a few times, sometimes, and when I thought I was pretty enough, I would walk the whole city in a delirious luxury of time and space, down East 2nd, and up A to Tompkins. Books in my backpack, cigarettes, and a bottle of water; I would wander in the easy May twilight for hours, the city smelling so good and sweet, flowers and piss and cinders, and amazement after amazement passing by. I stopped in at bookstores and read standing up, wandered my favorite blocks, sat on stoops, taking a break to smoke.

I had all the time in the world and all the amusement I could handle staring at everything around me. Seeing so many people up so late—walking, dropping into stores, taking the subway— was still so new to me, and half the time I didn't know how to behave. No one had shown me yet how to pass people on the sidewalk, talk to kids hanging out on the stoop, deal with men following me and hissing. Where I had grown up, there was nothing but industrial wasteland for miles. You could walk for hours, with no one else on the streets. It was so precious that in New York, people were allowed to sell books on blankets in the streets, sell weed, hang out in the dry fountain, cover the trains with graffiti and the lampposts with cracked mosaics of junk.

Smelling like Night Queen or Egyptian Musk, those sweet oils that girls of color my age bought in five-dollar vials on the street, I would feel my thighs brushing against each other as I walked, feel my beauty out on that street. I would practice. How to stare into the eyes of assholes til they dropped their gaze, or pick my nose and eat it, or scream "Fuck off!" or, the hardest, how to truly ignore it and not ever give anything away. Private space in this city was small and expensive, so I had to learn to make my private space in the six inches around my body.

There were hardly ever any bathrooms I could sneak into without having to buy something; it was a strict bag-check and customers-only world. Still, sometimes I could manage to rip off books in my knapsack or my coat after standing for hours in the aisles of the Strand or Tower Records or Barnes & Noble, waiting for the perfect moment when I could walk out with the Burroughs or Califia tucked inside.

The air, the streets, the people touched me all over. I kept my eyes on some of them, flirted, looked away. I couldn't find anyone to touch me, but in the meantime the air did, the world did.

Maybe there have always been hermit femmes coming into

adulthood who dress up for themselves and walk the streets, practice being pretty, smell booze and subway and lilac and cherry blossoms, loll on the richness of the city on the first day of spring. There have always been femmes getting grown in that narrow sweet space of being young, femme, and free. Maybe there have always been survivor femmes who paint on makeup and clothes, the sharp line of a tight miniskirt.

The books say we do this because it is the only way we know how to be beautiful, and that may be true. But I think there is something else, something about practicing hard beauty with a new room of our own, a door that locks, bare thighs, and a glare, practicing choosing who to let touch us, practicing letting no one touch us.

I was exhausted sometimes, when I finally came back to my apartment, climbed the five storeys, and undid the four locks. I would fall onto the twin mattress on the floor and doze, flip through my books, dream. I had been doing hard work, bringing myself to the sidewalk, learning how to appropriate and enjoy the street, how to bring myself into being.

Every cell of my body. Naked and tough, something new and beautiful, adorned. Learning these streets and how to walk down them. Learning how to find red silk in a bargain bin, to tighten straps, to walk. To meet the eyes. To swish my ass, to insist on the pleasure of thighs brushing together, glaring, *I will fucking kill you if you look at me.* I would fall into bed, exhausted.

There were still days, many days, where my body escaped me, flew away into gray dust, dead meat gray. I stroked it, but couldn't feel. But on the days when I wrapped her in red silk ribbons, the simple joy of a plum nipple, slight and hard under the thin strap of a black tank top, my hair curling out wild—years before I had the grown brown girls' lexicon of how to groom and polish—on those days, I rubbed salve on my brown silk thighs, built a delicate and tough girl skeleton to rise from.

31. Spinster

Everything in my family has taught me that it's safer to be a happy spinster than to try and love anybody. And, let's be real, when you look at the entire white colonialist capitalist ableist patriarchy, you don't see a whole lot that looks that great in terms of love and romance for surviving queer Black and brown femmes. Not a whole lot.

I want to do a PhD looking at June's and Audre's love affairs.

There are no happy memories of romance in my mom's archive. Everyone is married to an asshole and trying to survive it. My great aunt Stascia got knocked up by and married to a mill owner's son, who beat her and filled her with child after child. Between the chemicals from the shoe factory and constant estrogen from pregnancy, she got breast cancer and died in her thirties. My grandma is married to a drunk asshole. My great auntie Helen has no children and a nice husband whom I barely remember, her own small house, and is the happiest of all of the sisters. My father's mother was married off to a first cousin when in her early thirties, under protest, and continues to have affairs and hold her tiny, drunk husband in contempt. It is widely believed that my father is the product of an affair, not of her lawfully wedded marriage.

And then there are my parents, whose marriage we've discussed.

If ever since I was a kid, all I wanted was to be alone and happy with my own apartment with a door that locked, if all I could remember was the locked box, closed windows, pulled blinds, and trap of their marriage, how could I also dare to dream love?

Being free was enough of a miracle.

I was thirty-seven before I finally got it that this is the legacy I am rolling around with.

But I want romance, too. I fall fucking hard. Between 1996 and 2005, with a year's break in there, I'm pretty knee-deep in partnerships with a cis queer boy and then a genderqueer boy. I want marriage. I like steady. I have a lot of wifey in me. I am a Taurus. I want to prove that the curse didn't hit. That not only can I fuck and feel it, but can be happy. I hold my lovers like a promise, a prize. Not alone.

But sometimes being alone is the sweetest thing. The delish happy of bucking all my stupid schoolmates and their stupid marriages. I am really fucking happy, is the secret. I have peace of mind, freedom, a million shoes, and plane tickets. Sometimes I want a steady. I want an unconventional partnership.

I admit this. After a long-ass fucking break.

My homegirls study how to get this.

It's queer Black and brown femme love work we do. Love labor. We are pursuing PhDs in how to get good, good love that's not bullshit.

I get it and then I lose it. I'm not hungry the way I was, but contemplative. I realize how much I have wanted this and not gotten it, realize how much it is branded in my heart that, to be happy, alone, and childless is a fucking gift that most women get brainwashed into relinquishing.

The psychic tells me that my kid is waiting for me. She can see her, real clear.

She says, "This will be healing for you."

I say, "I don't want to have a kid to heal me. That's what my mom did. It's fucked-up to have a kid for your own purposes. You have a kid to bring a person into the world, love them hard. So they can add to the story."

She says, "You're not going to do it like your mom did, but it's gonna heal you anyway."

32. Shit Calms Down

There's this bit in *The Courage to Heal*, the very last part, where it says something like: "At some point, your life will stabilize. You will find that incest is no longer the only focus of your life."

It's the shortest section in the book.

It doesn't exactly say what the hell that part of your life will look like. But in my mind it was a picture I'd had in my head as a kid, which I never quite knew how I was going fit into, of a woman in an apartment serving dinner to her beautiful family, with an overlay of what happens when someone gets raped or dramatically remembers her abuse on a soap opera—a nice pastel therapy office, a nice lady counselor who is concerned, some crying, some uplifting music, and six weeks later, everything is fine and normal again.

Nice. But I couldn't see myself in it. Couldn't see how I was going to become That Woman. Me, with my basement apartment in a brick semi-detached on Davenport owned by Huong, who I'd met doing telemarketing. She was younger than me, her dad ran a corner store in Parkdale, done an engineering degree at Ryerson, and bought this house with her student loans, and was pretty easygoing if I "forgot" to pay the rent for a couple weeks.

There was this period. After I broke up with Rafael, after I got the ability to work, after I got my landed immigrant status, and an OHIP and SIN cards, after I got a bank account, and two jobs for $9.25 an hour, then one for $17. After I'd not been late on rent for a while, after I'd started fucking again, with some success, after nobody had been hitting or screaming at me, there had been no encounters with the law. There had been no thin beige yellow letters from Immigration.

My lover Jules told me that when we first started dating, that she thought I was an older lady with my shit together because I was twenty-six, had a couple non-profit, community-type jobs, read poetry at open mics, had my own place and some jeans without holes in them.

After I met Jules, shit never got like that sentence in *The Courage to Heal*, but it did calm the fuck down for a while, even though we hooked up exactly one month and five days after 9/11, a time that could be called anything but calm.

It was never that calm kind of quiet. It was the two of us sharing one Mystic CD, staying in bed basically for six months without changing the sheets even though she had one pair (they were black), having all the seven-year-olds across the street screaming "Get a room!" at us, smoking a pack a day of Benson & Hedges out the window, her making me strawberry crêpes with whipped cream, walking the railroad tracks and fucking in the abandoned truck with POOR graffed on the side, bonding over growing up broke, her making me mix tapes with Ms.

Dynamite and the Pogues singing "Dirty Old Town," wearing each other's clothes, fucking til everything was raw, me fisting her til she somersaulted off the edge of the bed. I got cervical dysplasia from smoking a pack a day and her fisting me once a day and both of us living off of one two-egg homefry breakfast, one boneless chicken roti with extra pepper on the inside and six cups of coffee a day diet plus 9/11 and working at the abortion clinic and the feminist rape crisis line, but even when she fucked me so hard there was blood to her elbow, I didn't want her to stop.

I didn't turn into a pastel lady with a daytime-drama haircut, and neither did she. It was more like going to Zellers to buy towels and sheets. It was her quitting video porn to hustle a youth worker job at the shelter where she used to be a client. Both of us deciding we wanted to be a little less broke. It was us making a parka pact with our friend Lorraine, after she declared: "Guys, we live in Toronto. A leather jacket and four hoodies isn't enough. Let's get real winter coats. It'll make our quality of life go up big time." It was a little less bone alone, a little less all flashback all the time. Calmness was exotic. The same girlfriend was exotic. Getting a matching towel set from Zellers for Christmas from her mother was exotic.

Four years went by like that, and if they were boring sometimes, it was the boredom my body was craving. Smokes and sleeps and taking two hours to crawl out of bed to make coffee, the same body in the bed next to me, winter and spring and summer and fall. My body craved it like you crave twelve hours of sleep after a lifetime of none.

Those years, we had sex and boredom and meeting her mom and Christmases and birthdays and fights we didn't know how to resolve and mix CDS. I started throwing queer-of-color spoken-word shows in abandoned grocery stores. I started writing grants. I taught writing to queer and trans youth for the first time. I published a chapbook. I got asked to publish my book. We moved in together. I went to New York to live for three months. We fought terribly because I wanted to quit my remaining two day a week non-profit job and be an artist full time and go to MFA school, even though going back to America and college scared the shit out of me, and me going to get a Masters when she still didn't even have a community college degree scared the shit out of her. We broke up.

But in those years, things did normalize, they just never got normal. They might've stopped being all crisis all the time, but I couldn't stop thinking about what incest and childhood sexual abuse, about colonial rape and internalized racism, what they do. What they are. How the story of my family kept speaking in me.

And maybe this is the story we need to write. If the story of surviving abuse, of being queer, isn't about getting to normal as the end goal. Isn't just sheets and towels and a long, quiet, Valium calm. Isn't disaster and death and everything we ran from either. Isn't anything we could've predicted, isn't anything predictable. What comes after the disaster we keep surviving every day?

33. Precious

When we lie on your bed, 3:39 a.m. West Philly Saturday night, you play with my hair, knit your fingers through my scalp, tease out each curl, follow its curve. You do it like you could do it forever. Without words, I know that you are loving that I have pretty desi girl hair, hair like your auntie's, dressed with oil, hair like your grandma had before the advent of The Bun.

After a while I ask, "Have you had a lot of South Asian femme girlfriends?"

"Once, in college, but it was real casual." There's a pause. Then you say, "I bet you've had lots of South Asian trans boyfriends. I mean, there's so many of us."

"Yeah. You, Kumaran, Subhash and, uh ..."

"There's that one guy in Massachusetts, but he only dates white girls."

I crack the fuck up and dig my hands into your sweet chai belly, the space I can touch between the boy shorts and T-shirt you keep on.

I'm not thinking of the other lover. The one I only recently started referring to as "my ex," recently as in this weekend. The one who is sleeping right now in her tighty-whities and

T-shirt in a bed I helped pick out. The one I started dating after a strict six-year "I only date queer POC" policy morphed into, "Just because she's a queer woman of color doesn't mean she's not an asshole." The one who cracked jokes as sarcastic as me, came from as fucked-up, dying, blue-collar town as me, grew up on hip-hop and her mama's welfare revolution. You know, we could love, fuck, and fight, and she never turned into a white ally nightmare.

We could love, fuck, and fight, and we did. And I told myself it didn't matter. That it was a surprise. That she loved *Monsoon Wedding* as much as I did. That she was the only white girl-friend my girls had met that they could stand, and more than that, enjoy.

But this was the one thing she could never do.

How could she say, "You have pretty desi hair"?

No matter how fine she thought I as, how the hell could she think, *damn, you're a fine brown girl.*

Want to know my dirtiest secret?

I never thought anyone South Asian would find me sexually attractive. Never ever, in all those years of going to Funkasia every month and Basement Bhangra whenever I was in New York, not in all those year of queer woman of color everything. I figured the only ones who would be into me would be assholes hung up on light-skinned women, or the ones who like to say "Mixed-race people are so beautiful!"—and why the hell would I date them?

When I was at Funkasia and Basement, beauty knocked me over. A swarm of hundreds of gorgeous desi girls, swirling and grinding. Whether they were from Chittagong or San Fernando, Batticaloa or Mumbai, those girls rocked perfect eyebrows, big almond eyes, and Zeenat Aman booty. I might have had the booty, might've even had the eyes, but I also had hairy armpits and my mother's Ukrainian potato face. I'd grown up looking at her powder blue CoverGirl eyeshadow, then at white girls in black leather. I figured no one saw me. Brown, sure, but never desi without an explanation, and never that kind of knock-you-over desi femme. I hadn't gone to the same threading-waxing-sari-and-churridor-shopping-samosa-making-good-biodata school of crazy desi high femme-hood, filled with girls named Twinkle and Pepsi, and I figured I could never catch up.

Your fingers run through my hair, 3:39 a.m., West Philly night. You have no question that I am a pretty desi girl. Even better than a film star or your hot cousin, I'm a hot femme who can play with your ass and fuck you in the men's room at the club.

I know you could be an asshole.

I know we could disagree about everything tomorrow.

But right now, you pull each curl like it's precious,

and I am more beautiful than I've ever been before.

34. The Palace of Words

If we believe the story that I chose to believe—the story that led me out of my childhood—my mother touched me when I was a kid, a really little kid, and something split. Something really big split.

And when I split, there was a place in me that stayed in the place before there were words.

And when I split, there was another place that learned language in self-defense. Words and words and words and words.

In one story my mother tells, I speak for the first time at six months. I say the word "Mama," angrily. I am pissed. She is going away. When she tells the story, she laughs. "You were so angry!" I can see myself standing up in my crib. It's just an image; maybe it didn't happen.

In another story, I learn to read young at Montessori School, where I'm on financial aid, at the age of three. I teach myself. By four, I am reading. Reading reading reading, above grade level, always. Hungry. When I'm twelve, I find out how many books you can check out of the library at once. It's fifty. I regularly have that. Big stacks of plastic wrapped crinkly chunky hardcovers, all over the floor. Books with condoms that protect their big broad shoulders from abuse, carried in my army backpack, stacked up in big falling-over stacks on the floor, shoved under my bed.

The story crosses another story, which is the story where I didn't know how to talk; I was that kid who cried at the drop of a hat. The kid who was sensitive and so mature. The kid who cried and cried and cried if somebody looked at her funny, who hid behind her mama's legs, who would get seized by a vomitous sort of panic when some adult said "hi" to me. I was the kid who didn't really have friends til college. This shit is funny now, and nobody believes me that I used to have a hard time talking, because now I talk and talk, I tell stories, I perform on stage, I cannot shut the fuck up even though I am also a good listener. But the words Shy and Sensitive and Mature and Adult-like dotted my body when I was growing up. I was much more comfortable with books and the inside of my head.

There is a part of me that still remembers how to talk without words, that knows what consciousness was like before words. I could sum up a thought with images, colors, and meaning far beyond anything as gross as words.

Maybe what happened made me get stuck there. And maybe being a writer has to do with learning words in self-defense, wanting the world, wanting to tell, yet being loyal to the place inside that is beyond words.

When I am grown, there are times when language leaves me. When I am hurt badly through breakup or crisis, through sex that triggers, through being down at the bottom of that hole where shit whispers *kill yourself*. I am small and scared, sitting in that hole. I can't talk, but I am also blissful. I enjoy being that austere child who disdains anything as crude as verbal language. I'd much rather use light or sound or beats or color to express my thoughts. When I find a lover who is also a psychic abuse survivor, who does preverbal too, it brings me joy.

There are times where I want to be the person my mom sometimes told me we were, space aliens from another planet that didn't need people.

I learned how to speak and write in self-defense.

Words are a palace of heaven.

35. Feed the Ache: 2010

Sometimes I feel like my life's work is one long meditation on how things fall up and out and down, fall no matter how hard you try. My life's work is a return to the splayed out inside of a girl-on-girl broken heart.

No matter how many safe words, accountability strategies, I-statements, and non-violent communication workbooks, commitment to each other, to building life-long, no matter what, no promise. Just the promise of her to you. The one you bet your life on. She can write a performance piece about how God picked you out for each other before you were born and perform it for 300 people, and that doesn't mean that six months later she isn't sending you the long email, the long chain of words that shows how well she knows you, she knows how to destroy you.

At the Femme Conference, the 2010 one, the theme is every girl who's broken the inside of your heart. This is the femme con where we start to cry two minutes into Kate Bornstein's speech as she talks about what it takes to survive to make it to femme; a whole conference chamber of femmes ruining their eye makeup. Everyone here has a story to tell of the femme she loved so much, more than anything, gave her rent money to, conceived their children together. Femme family. And then one day you woke up, and she just hated your guts. You didn't know who she was anymore. She hated you, hated you utterly, and you hadn't done a damn thing. I loved her so much, I loved her better than anything, sobs girl into my shoulder.

I always say, "I can't fuck femmes. It'd be a fucking mess. I need my girls to be who I don't date, it's safer."

But it's a fucking mess anyway. We break each other's hearts even when we don't date each other.

My mama raped me. That's a fact.

My mama almost killed me. Ran from her since little, long shadow.

I came out when I was twelve, but I didn't fuck another person who called themself female in any way til I was twenty-six. I chose queer masculinity my whole life. It was a walled garden. It was a place where I thought my femme was elevated, seen, cherished. It was not titties. It was not pussy. Titties scared the hell out of me.

Women scared the hell out of me.

You can't get angry at women. They'll kill you. They'll love you better than anyone. They'll kill you.

When I was thirty-five, I lost my femme virginity in a darkened conference room at the Oakland Marriott. The lights are off and "Promiscuous Girl" is blaring and it's true: femmes know how to fuck other femmes because we are femmes who like to get fucked.

I am between two thick brown femmes, and it's the hottest

thing I've ever done. It's enough, it's more than enough. I pull her hair, she pulls mine. We give into each other's need. My brain blows out my ears. I feel like I put my face in jesus's pussy, and I'm born again. We are all ache and skill and need to fuck each other as the sluts we are, beyond shame. Would this solve everything, if we just fucked each other? Straddled thick or skinny brown thighs blessed the center of each other's chests?

We are in this work until we win or we die. *We all we have, sweetness, all we have.* And when you get so close like blood thrumming is to vein's skin, she pulls out the knife to cut you out and open when you hurt her on purpose or on accident. Anything you do affects her whole life. So she cuts you up and out.

No easy solutions. No promises. Just the deep long memory. Just the prayer of compassion. Sister, star. I want your light to be as big as mine and mine to be as big is yours. If I shine, it's because of you. I want us both to.

36. The Opening

Femme sexuality is about voracious desire for which no apologies are necessary.

—*Ann Cvetkovitch*, AN ARCHIVE OF FEELINGS

1.

"You're so open right now. I could almost fist you," my lover says. I say "making love" with this one without irony. There are many moments when we make love and kiss, and it's sacred, it's hovering spirits inhabiting and flying over our bodies; it's making love with the psychic incest-survivor crazy who is a grownup after a lot of therapy and meditation who I found, waded in a river and prayed for.

They have four fingers inside me. They have big hands. I am all the way open. The day before my period. New moon in Pisces, and I've been crying from the gut all week. *All the way love. All the way open to you.* It doesn't hurt. It's not hard. I am opening. I come a series of high and open. I will keep opening for you. I make this joyful choice.

2. femme like a fist

I walk down the street. My face closed like a fist. I pump my hands hard. I walk fast. I stomp. I have my sunglasses on. Sometimes I strut or sashay. Sometimes I smile, say, "Hey, how you doing." Do the nod. But mostly, I walk fast. I walk don't-fuck-with-me. I walk I-will-kill-you-if-you-look-at-me. It protects me. I don't get fucked with on the street. I look too crazy and full of rage for that shit to happen.

3. sick rock

When I am sick, I get harassed more.

This has to do with the visible symbols of disability—my cane, my shaky walk, my sitting down, the look of pain or exhaustion on my face. But much more than those obvious visual cues, it is how I am not impervious. I am open, translucent. I am not impenetrable. The disabled, crazy femme body is touchable.

Men knock on my window as I am trying to find a parking spot, disabled pass visible, as is my flaring, tired energy field. As a femme witch, every step of my razor-sharp ass is a spell to keep harassers away. When I am sick, I am more open to *la facultad*, the ability to see that Gloria Anzaldúa spoke of.

One night, I'm at the Red Baraat show. A man comes up to me and starts screaming at me because I don't recognize him, yelling at me, "What's wrong with you? Oh, you remember white people but not brown people?" When I try to explain that I have a chronic illness that affects my long-term memory, and I honestly have no idea who he is, he sneers, "You expect me to believe that?" I have to talk myself over the bridge on the way home. I am crying wide open, with no control.

4. vaginismus

clench hard tight no fuck you ouch nothing nothing nothing goes in nothing. No pelvic exams. I imagine sex that feels good to get through them. "This shouldn't hurt" looks, doc after doc.

Years of wanting to get fucked; the erotics of it, opening, being filled, the pleasure upon being filled. I could feel it, how good it would feel to get fucked. But then, when it did, it didn't feel like anything. Or it hurt. It felt numb and it hurt and I faked it like I'd learned how to do from queer porn. Sometimes I bled from my cervix. I would tell lovers not to worry about it. My cervix was friable; that's what the doctors said, but she was also speaking. She was clear, she didn't want to be touched.

5. girl body grown

in order to be touched, I built a shell
in order to be touched, I built a false body
in order to be touched, I made up a femme body
like I made up altars
my femme body was always there, rushing skirts, how I stayed
in love with color
and she was also something I made up, steel and lace corset
over skeleton, that could stand to be touched

The real body was curled up in a lean-to, in a hoodie. She was making a fire outta sticks. She was not draping her body with dresses that curved and invited touch. She was simultaneously almost naked and would murder you for touching her, ever. For even thinking about it.

6.

"Femme vulnerability is not just active because of the work of actively soliciting a lover's desire. It is active because it is work. Being good in bed as a femme meant communicating my responses. Moaning, talking, breathing, shifting, letting her know the effect her lovemaking had on me, letting her know what I wanted." —*Amber Hollibaugh*

It was work to let them into my body, to decide how far. To create the conditions where letting my lover in wasn't just a one-way street with no stop sign once we started driving. To know I could ask for a pause, for a drink of water, communicate that I was young or disassociated. To learn to know the moment when my body started to shift, when I didn't enjoy that particular stroke of tongue.

For years I thought, a femme bottom—what is more common, what is more despised? Than a girl with her legs open. Wanting something. Just wanting.

I didn't come up with this idea on my own. The whole world told me it was true. The whole world told me that there is nothing more common and stupid than someone feminine of center with their legs open, wanting something more than a kick or a curse.

*But what if there is nothing more precious than a femme with
their legs open?
If our opening is a prayer it is for a world where opening
without rape is possible*

walk back

*wade in the water
choose. every second. I choose to stay here. I learn to stay here.
I choose to open
every single second led to this.*

37. Mama, Three Ways

....

one

mama reading books stack hammock library smile telling me
I'm beautiful just not the kind they know about around here
mama driving us to Cambridge driving us to bookstores and
poetry mama helping me allowing me to go to poetry camp to
young writers camp mama being okay every single time I cried
mama the best friend close one of the best parts of my childhood the thing the person I would've said I loved the most who
kept me alive.

....

two

mama who I got away from when I was in New York I was finally
away raw eighteen all hell has broken loose inside me don't go
to bed before six a.m. each night the whole year feel like I'm
going crazy, I am crazy, I can't tell anybody, any school counselor, what the inside of my head feels like, it'll be Prozac Xanax
it'll be back home failure not let me out again you got one ticket

to ride, kid, don't blow it, the last thing I want is to be back in that house. If I get back in that house I'm never gonna be let out I'm gonna be some famous loser trapped fighting with her folks forever til they die. Everything feels like a TV program.

One time I am walking tripping on acid with my nineteen-year-old blond Pre-Raphaelite indie-rock boyfriend, and I lose my memory of the neighborhood I walk every day, it's like I've never seen any of those buildings before. Totally fresh new just images that are floating in front of my eyes. No context. A little blip in the brain. My brain is definitely a little weird, but mama is who I got away from; she's not there and my body is just starting to come down from being surveyed, to see what it feels like, to tentatively reach out and touch the sides of my body. Walls; they are there.

....

three

Mama and me fighting, not quite the same way you fought with your mama, or maybe it was.

Mama cutting all my hair off the last time I went home for Christmas, the next to last time I went home.

Mama telling me, when her cancer came back, and I told her she could do Reiki, "I don't know about all that. The doctor told me they got all the cancer. I don't need chemo, but I want it anyway. I want to feel clean inside."

Mama writing me a postcard in her Palmer Method

handwriting—so precise it was like it was engraved from the fingers of the meanest nun ever—telling me she'd consider forgiving me if I got on my knees and begged her.

Mama telling me, "I don't need to hit you. I just stop loving you and you fall right in line."

Mama, other people need music and friends. "We don't need that."

My mama, I asked her once if she missed having friends. She paused, thought about it, and said, "I have a rich inner life."

you telling me what a nice ass I had

you not letting me walk off the block

you timing how long it took me to walk to the mailbox and back

you enraged and crying when I was forty-five minutes late driving home from an Amnesty International youth conference in Boston. You had called the cops, the hospital, and the fire department.

you calling every day

you crying and cursing and weeping

you telling me that if we talk to therapists, they'll take me away

you telling me: you can't go for a walk there, you'll get raped

you crying spasmodically, "You are killing me, you are killing me!" because I walked down to the drugstore, because I walked downtown to the library

this is my big rebellion: walking

mama writing me with one all bold, all caps letter and

thirty pages of a children's book

mama not talking to any of us for three days. The sun going out.

mama telling me I was crazy and they weren't fighting, nothing was happening, we hadn't had that discussion, I must be remembering it wrong. I know you were not a monster. I see you in my own face.

Worst daughter.

Best daughter.

I changed this, for us, mama.

Rest.

38. Multigenerational

When I was a kid, one of my mom's favorite places to visit in the summer was the graveyard in Webster, Mass.

Sometimes, we'd go to the one where our family members were buried, but often we'd go to "the owners" graveyard. Webster had segregated cemeteries for everyone who lived in Webster, who had anything to do with a mill. There was the Jewish cemetery and the Irish-Polish cemetery (both were Catholic, so had intermarried a lot, and it didn't make sense for their cemeteries to be separate). The Black cemetery and the Indian cemetery were near the small Nipmuc rez. And then there was the owners' cemetery, the fancy one where the Slaters and the other mill-owners' families buried their dead.

My mom was a schoolteacher, when she had work. In 1980, 20,000 teachers had been laid off from the Massachusetts public school system and there was a hiring freeze for everything but special ed. We lost the art and music departments years before the '90s hit and everyone else was talking cuts and recession. She had had to figure some things out. My father had been a personnel manager at WPI, a local engineering college. Then he got a promotion. Then he got fired. Then his work was tenuous.

My mother had kept her part-time work at home, correcting mail-order correspondence business courses for the American Management Company. She had been a management consultant with two of her friends. That company had folded. She had gotten hired at Worcester's Hasidic community's yeshiva to teach English and history when I was maybe in fifth grade. She had gotten hired to teach at my school when I went into ninth. She worked teacher's hours: 5:30 a.m. wake-up, 7:15 a.m. arrival, work til three, buy groceries, make dinner, correct papers in front of the TV, bed by 9:30, more work on the weekends. (When she asked me if I ever thought about teaching, I shuddered.) But she had the summers off.

In the summers, she liked to do genealogical research, specifically central Massachusetts labor history.

Mom wanted to be a writer.

She wanted to write young adult novels and kids' books about suffrage and labor unions, about working-class, white family history. That's part of why we went to the library so often, why she grilled her own mother for information and wrote down her stories. It's why she got so excited when I wanted to do my own family history projects. We would go down to the owners' cemetery, my mom would take notes, and I would hang out there in that tiny, abandoned place, with its eight-foot-tall spires of granite memorializing dead rich men who had made money off my great aunties' fingers. It was abandoned and forgotten. Where were the scions of the Slater empire now? Had they lost it all when the factories went south to Kentucky, where there were no unions? Were they at my school?

The graveyard was overgrown, lush with Massachusetts June and July and August. Big, wet green grass and tiny little purple vetch flowers, Sweet Williams and morning glories, orange tiger lilies gone wild, and juicy phlox with bees sucking the nectar from inside the purple kiss of the flowers. I would sit with my back propped up by a gravestone, tall stack of library books next to me, scratching words into a notebook.

Sometimes we would visit my grandma who lived on Social Security in an apartment complex for broke old people out in the middle of a field on the edge of Webster. It was near the roadhouse where the Harley bikers hung out, a ten-minute drive from downtown with its used-to-be Woolworths, its fading murals of textile mills, its Kmart and five-cent savings and loan where we'd go in and manage her money, its Friendly's and supermarket.

Sometimes, my mother would tell me her stories:

We'd drive by the old brick red triple decker on School Street that I remembered from when I was younger. My grandad's woodshop in the basement, all the vises and other tools, the top two floors rented out, plastic on the old couch. Towers of empty Blue Bonnet margarine tubs for tupperware. Stop for a minute.

My mom would tell me stories.

She went to school at the local Catholic school. One time, the nuns broke her little brother Johnny's leg, and he'd had to walk home on it. She officially dropped out of the Church when she was eighteen, but she really dropped out much earlier, when she realized that they would never let her be an altar boy. Both her dad and mom hated her because she was a girl. She'd been a National Merit Finalist in high school, and her mother had said, "What's that? That's nice." It didn't mean anything because she was a girl. Everything was for the boys. My mother graduated from high school with all As, a National Merit Finalist, and she went to work as a typist in the office of one of the local mills. In one of those miraculous stories that is too good to be true but happens sometimes, her high school English teacher came into the mill one day and saw her there. He said, "This won't do," pulled some strings, and got her into Worcester State, the teacher's college. Got her financial aid. Got her out of there. How she lived in a house with other girls going to State, but she still liked books better. She didn't really make friends at the college. Liked to smoke out her window and read Sartre better.

Her maiden name was Helen McGilvrey. She was a working-class white girl, a traumatized, intellectual shy girl who thought she was ugly, who was bold yet couldn't speak. She dreamed of moving to Boston but couldn't; she was too scared. She got her own apartment and taught school anyway, and was the only girl in her high school class who didn't get married right after graduation or get pregnant and drop out. The girls she'd grown up with looked down on her—she was a spinster. But she was happy in her little working-class, bachelor girl apartment, buying takeout from one of the diners instead of cooking, saving up money to go on one-week solo cheap trips to Ireland to fish, to Paris, when no working-class girl did that. Nobody's girl, nobody's housewife. Alone and safe and lonely.

She told me about my grandfather, Charlie McGilvrey, the

master mechanic and foreman, who drank every day. I never met him because he was diagnosed with liver cancer when I was six months old. The doctors told him he wouldn't be able to drink anymore and he had a heart attack that day. She told me she was pretty sure he willed himself into it—that he couldn't imagine living without a bottle.

My mama tried to tell me all the stories she hadn't been able to tell. She told me that both her parents had hit her. About her father chasing her around the house with his belt. Sometimes, the silence would get thick and her voice would trail off. She told me things that she didn't need to use words to tell. I knew. I knew what probably happened, what had to have happened, besides hitting.

So my mother gave her daughter enough food and enough books and never hated her daughter for being smart. She coached me to get a full scholarship like other girls get groomed for a boyfriend or prom, I got library books, a scrimped-for college fund, heard, "Don't worry about these people, they're stupid." She never told me that I was stupid. I was "better than" and "getting out" and "different."

She said: "When you get to college, you can have friends. You're not going to be stuck in Worcester like your cousins. You got one ticket to ride, kid, don't blow it. Leave this place behind. And life is short, so you better go out like a goddamn meteor."

She told me, "I tell you the things they wouldn't let me talk about. When you grow up, you will be the writer. Tell them. You'll write this down like I couldn't. Tell the world."

But when I grew up and started to want to tell all of it,

everything, she said, "They'll kill you. I'll kill you. Move back home. Move in with me."

My mama's broken heart.

My mom never got published.

She got cancer instead.

The psychic tells me: "You're the one who breaks everything, who stops it, who changes it all."

38.5. Made It Home: 2012

I am thirty-six and have arrived here. Life has taken me to a big, crooked house on Stuart Street in Southwest Berkeley, to the crip, queer, femme, majority of color house of my dreams. It is my good dream. A Taurus survivor girl, I dreamed this big house full of color, burnt orange and magenta walls, bookshelves spilling over, notices tacked to the fridge and bulletin board of parties and benefits, childhood and current photos of housemates hugging on each other wallpapering the fridge. My pictures tend to look like this. In nine of ten of my Facebook photos, I am hugging on some friend, lover, fam. My photos shout, over and over again: I made it, I am not alone, I am loved, loved, loved.

My house has a big messy garden with curvy girl beds, a magnolia tree and a camellia bush, plum and fig and walnut trees. Big sacks of food line the pantry shelves, ready for the end of the world, and all of our various weird cars are out front. It is the safe house of my best dreams, the Samuel Delany-style compound where housemates run in and out, cooking greens, checking in about lovers and weeks and mental and physical health, throwing money for food in the house jar, cooking from the thirty-six pack of free-range eggs on the kitchen table I bought. All the windows open.

I am thirty-six, and I have landed in and co-created this femme of color survivor home. And this is why I can write to my father at Christmas and be happy when he writes me back the same week, sending me a card in a shiny gold envelope. Because I am his daughter, and we both have excellent taste and love shiny and gold. Because we are both gay. That man who taught me how to find a Brooks Brothers suit on quadruple markdown in a T.J. Maxx. This house is where I can fall in love with someone who can meet me, touch me, who is not afraid to claim me as their lover in public. This is why I am prettier than I was two years ago, with some white hair and the beginning of brown girl, what-the-fuck lines between my eyebrows. I am lovely. I made my way home. I made this home.

I'll tell you a secret. Sometimes I stop and close my eyes and send all these pictures of my life back to the kid I was, who is still back there, trying to survive. Prayer is activism.

I tell her: this is waiting, waiting. It doesn't get better (but it did), it just changes. I pray it to her, promise her, say, "Stay alive. This is what's waiting for you. You will make it come to be."

39. Redemption Song

So, if this isn't a typical abuse story, can we not have a typical abuse story ending?

You will study this for clues and use it as a roadmap, an atlas, a Googlemap with the "Avoid highways" option clicked. Know that there are so many worthy stories, so many tiny points on my life, that did not get translated into words. At the age of thirty-seven, I have stable housing, paychecks, money in the bank, renters' insurance, a lover, friends, acclaim, a cool twenty-two-year-old, hundred-dollar car, brown skin, and an amazing and mundane life.

It's eleven days til the end of the year. I write all day, get in my car, go to the gym, come home and eat, have a meeting, and read through old emails looking for the first one my lover ever sent me. I sleep later than I planned because my body aches from fibromyalgia, but I shower, dress, drive into the clean, cold light to the fancy place where my friend and I get fancy doughnuts and coffee because her lover worked there. They have broken up, and he doesn't work there any more, but the computer malfunctions and the waiter is so distracted with his new tattoo and smartphone that I get fancy yogurt and granola, a doughnut, and a latte for free. There are flowers curving up, new fishnets my roommate bought me for Christmas, and the sky is incredibly blue, sunshot and bright after days of the grayest dull northern California winter.

The end of a world supposedly happens in three days. I don't believe it. Or I do. This whole year, nothing came according to plan, so it is no wonder that I have a hard time making plans for next year—me whose entire life has been drafted according to plans.

Seven years ago, I broke up with my partner of four-and-a-quarter years, quit my terrible day job at the eviction prevention hotline, and decided, after much terror and saving money, to be a full-time writer with no trust fund. I had my lists. I was going to publish books and travel the world and start organizations and move back to the US and go to grad school, even though I was sure I would hate it. I had all these marvelous one- and five-year plans.

It's not just about escaping a terrible childhood. It's about figuring one's way through a future that is beautiful and utterly unpredictable. Whether you choose safety or stick your thumb out, you are not guaranteed happiness or calm. You get bored of your husband. You stare horrified at your eviction notice. It all falls apart, and then it is a miracle. We don't understand it. We make the same mistakes over and over again.

Stakes are high and nothing is certain—witness foreclosures and mudslides. Witness elders falling off the edge. Witness how our community kills when they don't understand disability or how to make things right. I do not leave myself out of this assessment.

You find me here. Now I am thirty-seven, the same age my mother was when she gave birth to me. Giving birth to this pile of words instead.

There is the word "home" tattooed on my chest between my breasts in red brown ink the color of Sri Lankan earth. The word "lucky" tattooed on my right wrist. This body, the only home I'll ever own. On loan.

Let me tell you a story, darling *kunju*. It's the oldest one in the book, or before books. A girl runs away from home and tries to get free. On the way, she takes a bus, hops a border, loses her hair, her clothes, her everything.

There are twists and turns, and you want to know, will she get out? Maybe she is you, the girl you were when you left home, stopped talking to your parents, were such a horrible daughter. You never could do anything right, could you? You did yourself right. You ran away. You were never seen again. You were a ghost girl floating around the city. Your spirit is a shred that hovers around these skyscrapers. She's still here. Even if you think they didn't see your body flaming, it was flaming. It was there. It's still there.

Kick the trike pedal. Push off. You can feel this wind rush between your legs. You're riding that baby-blue trike standing up, picking up speed down the big hill. Your hair streams out behind you, tits hard. The city spreads her legs in front of you—your city. Trees and the secret gardens and alleyways, the lake, the smoggy horizon, the CN Tower, Kensington, the jails and the big mall, the dirty river and the airport. New York, Oakland, Colombo, the world; you are getting on an airplane and taking the fuck off.

You ran away to find freedom, and you found it. You made it. Now you gotta tell it. You gotta figure out how to tell the story.

Thanks and Acknowledgments

Thank you to every queer femme/of color/survivor/crip who has ever written their life.

Thank you to Alexis Pauline Gumbs, for so many reasons, but especially for writing your thesis, which shed new light for me on exactly how difficult and necessary the doing of ground-breaking feminist, queer of color publishing is, when June Jordan was doing it, and now. For inspiring me to write my heart out on this book with my freest brown girl writer self by all the ways you are your freest, most brilliant Black Queer Troublemaker Genius self. For giving me a writing retreat in your home, the Inspiration Station, where I picked up this book again in the summer of 2010.

Thank you to Lidia Yuknovitch, whose memoir *The Chronology of Water* showed me how to finish this book, seven years in, when I had almost given up. Thank you for showing me that I didn't have to write a narrative that went from point A to point B and that, in fact, it would be a waste of time. For writing the phrase, "a suitcase big enough to hold the rage of a girl."

Thank you to Audre Lorde for writing *Zami,* for blowing

open the container of memoir with queer Black feminist brilliance. Thank you to Gloria Anzaldúa, Randa Jarrar, Roxanne Dunbar-Ortiz, June Jordan, Ariel Gore, Minal Hajratwala, and many others for writing memoirs that were queer of color femme road maps and models for me.

Thanks to Amber Hollibaugh, who said yes to my being her intern when I stomped into her office at age twenty-one, who was one of my first femme mentors and whose book, *My Dangerous Desires: A Queer Girl Dreaming Her Way Home* inspired this one.

Thank you to Femmes of Color: A Transnational Solidarity Group, for being the best revolutionary non-sorority on the planet. I finished this book for you and with you in my heart. Thank you to Sick and Disabled Queers for being the best disability justice kin network I could ask for.

Thank you to Liz Latty for being a most excellent memoir writing partner, druncle femme, America's Foulest Gay Roadshow co-conspirator, travel companion to tiny hostels for writing retreats, Friday night gay yoga and burgers partner, best girl. Thanks for giving me Lidia. Thanks for being loud and wilding out with me and telling me that I could figure out how to write this book by doing it, and showing me by example.

Thank you to my home girls and bois, old girls, *thangatchis* and *akkas* in Toronto and elsewhere, who pushed me to finish this manuscript and who remember all these years. Lisa Amin, Sheila Battacharya, Sheila Bannerjee, Ishwar Persaud, Aruna Boodram, Eshan Rafi, Hari Malagayo Alluri, Rabea Murtaza, Amandeep Kaur, Arti Mehta, Rosina Kazi and Nicholas Murray,

Karene Silverwomyn, LeRoi Newbold, Sabera Esufeli, Jessica Mustachi, Farrah Khan, Jules Jordison, Zavisha Chromicz, Keisha Williams, and everyone from back in the day—I am accountable to you and wrote this for you.

Cherry Galette, Chanelle Gallant, Micha Cardenas, Tre Vasquez, Tina Zavitsanos, Luna Merbruja, Meg Day, Naima Lowe, Gesig Selena Isaac, Ellery Russian, Patty Berne, SB McKenna, Sham-e-Ali Nayeem, Minal Hajratwala, Manish Vaidya, Juliana Pegues, Joe Kadi, Bao Phi, Simi Kang, Robin Park, David Findlay, Nalo Hopkinson, Gabriel Teodros, Walidah Imarisha, mel g campbell, Neve Mazique, Stacie Milbern, Ryan Li Dahlstrom, Maya Chinchilla, Setarah Mohammed, Adrienne Maree Brown, V.S. Tobar, McKenzie Reynolds, Ejeris Dixon, Adrian Cole, Aaron Ambrose, Meliza Banales, Annah Anti-Palindrome, Leah Henderson, Fran Varian, Sabaa Westbrooks, Texta Queen, Amirah Mizrahi; all of you were and are inspirations and motivations for me to finish this fucking thing.

Deep, deep appreciation to Norcroft for being the writer's residency where this book started in 2005, and Fancyland for being the place where I figured out how to finish it ten years later. I remain in awe of these places with their gifts of demanding silence.

Thank you to Jess Hoffman and *Make/Shift* magazine for publishing some excerpts that became Pushcart Prize nominees in 2010. Thank you to Elokin Orton-Cheung for giving me a first place to read "The Punk Rock Kid of Color Clusterfuck" at Hotpot in May 2010; the screaming laughter gave me motivation to keep going.

Cristina Garcia's fall 2007 fiction writing workshop at Mills College redeemed grad school for me when I was ready to drop out after two weeks. Elmaz Abinadar's memoir class at Voices of Our Nations 2006 taught me more than I can say, as did the precious, never taken for granted writers of color community that VONA nurtures. Suheir Hammad's maestra teaching gave me tools that allowed me to enter into these stories when my body didn't know how to.

Without the Toronto family and queer/of color community art spaces—many of which no longer exist—that I lived and worked within from 1996 to 2007, I wouldn't have lived to grow up, let alone become a writer and have a career. Thank you from the bottom of my heart to Sister Vision Press, A Different Booklist, This Ain't The Rosedale Library, Toronto Women's Bookstore, Desh Pardesh, Mayworks, and Clit Lit, whose cultural work in the '90s and 2000s gave me room to breathe and speak and get good. And to the ass-kicking present: my Asian Arts Freedom School family, we are the ones, let's do this!

This book is also for many people who have died or with whom I am no longer in contact but who matter critically to the times depicted in this work. I especially want to remember the lives of Bobbie N. and Jim Campbell, who both passed in 2007, and David Melville and Will Munroe, who passed in 2010.

Thank you to Burntface, Gabriel Teodros, and Meklit Hadero, for recording the album *Earthbound* as the band Copperwire and giving me the music I listened to obsessively while I was writing the last chunk of this marathon. We built for this.

Thank you to Project Prepare, Sins Invalid, and to everyone

at every college who booked me for keeping me marginally employed as a chronically ill working artist with no trust fund, buying me time to finish this book. Thank you to The Shark Pit, Casa Maize, The Mixed Femme Bro Cave, and the Shrieking Shack, my homes for the final years of working on this book. Thanks to the Healing Babes for Justice, my Allied Media Conference family, healing justice and transformative justice comrades. Thank you to Vanissar Tarakali and Dori Midnight, my mentors in intuition and healing, for walking with me as I wrote this.

Thank you to Brian Lam, Susan Safyan, Gerilee McBride, and the entire team at Arsenal Pulp Press for saying yes, making me cry, and fighting to bring queer-of-color writing into the world. Thank you for believing in me and for the labor and art you poured into this book.

Finally, thank you to Jesse Manuel Graves for answering each other's witch of color love spell prayers, healing all the stuff I thought was broken for good, and transforming my life.

Many names and identifying details have been altered to protect people's privacy.

Dirty River was written on unceded and occupied Three Fires Confederacy, Mississauga of New Credit, Wiyot, Yurok, Miwok, Ohlone, and Lenape land.

Leah Lakshmi Piepzna-Samarasinha is a queer disabled femme writer and performer of Burgher/Tamil Sri Lankan and Irish/Roma ascent. The author of the Lambda Award-winning *Love Cake, Bodymap,* and *Consensual Genocide,* and co-editor of *The Revolution Starts At Home: Confronting Intimate Violence in Activist Communities,* her writing has been widely anthologized. She is the co-founder of Mangos With Chili, North America's touring queer and trans people of color cabaret, and is a lead artist with the disability justice incubator Sins Invalid.